Let Them Speak!

Woman's cry for freedom is heard to permeate all walks of life and culture, and must they fight for it to have it, they will!

Bruce Kele

authorHOUSE®

AuthorHouse™
1663 Liberty Drive
Bloomington, IN 47403
www.authorhouse.com
Phone: 1-800-839-8640

First published by AuthorHouse 12/11/2009

ISBN: 978-1-4490-1212-0 (sc)

Printed in the United States of America
Bloomington, Indiana

This book is printed on acid-free paper.

A Book that establishes from a biblical standpoint why a woman has as much right as the man, but with one exception!

Bruce Kele

Table of Contents

Personal Acknowledgement

When writing this book, there were many days that I would contemplate the thought of quitting and not taking another step further to complete the book, due to the nature of the content itself. The Lord would then speak to me about not being afraid to speak out in forms of writing and not to be deterred from the goal of compiling such a controversial study in the world of gender issues, Christianity, religion and culture since it was He who commanded me to do so.

From a one-year project, this became a six-year project for which I had dragged myself to accomplish, again because of "the nature of its content." Just because something's popular does not mean its right. I had to force myself to write what may be unpopular but what I believe to be the truth that the World needs to hear!

Koila, my beloved wife and the mother of my four lovely children, was a huge encouragement to the writing of this book. If it wasn't for her, I definitely wouldn't be able to even have the guts to get it into the hands of a waiting World.

My daughter Amy whom I praise very much, a spiritual general in the making has inspired me so much to go ahead with the writing of this book.

A couple good friends of mine who mean a lot to me and helped in partial editing whom I would like to acknowledge are: Merrily Shirey & Pamela Verebasaga. The third one is more than a friend, my mother who completed the editing process, along with my sister Clara.

About the Author

Bruce Kele was born and raised in the Republic of the Fiji Islands. In September of 2001 he moved with his wife and three kids to the United States of America, to pursue Biblical studies. Bruce has had another daughter since who was born in the United States of America. He has been pastor of two different Churches in the past fourteen years, but is in a transitional period of completing his studies in a Masters degree in Transformation leadership. He is a gifted teacher of the word of God and a motivational speaker.

I Am Woman

Oh Yes I am Wise but its Wisdom born of pain. Yes, I've paid the price but look how much I have gained. If I have to, I can do anything. I am strong (Strong) I am invincible (Invincible) I am Woman.

You can bend me but never break me, `cause it only serves to make me. More determined to achieve my final goal, And I come back even stronger not a novice any longer `cause you've deepen the conviction in my soul.

Partial chorus of song "I am Woman"

Artist: Helen Reddy

Introduction

It was the summer of 1999, I was amongst a group of older speakers designated to speak at a men's conference in a remote location out in the country. I was the youngest and was pastor of a church in the Fiji Islands in a small town twelve miles from the capital city, Suva. I was happily married with only one child and my wonderful wife was expecting a double blessing: twins.

That Thursday evening I drove my old, worn out 1988 Subaru about ten miles to this meeting where I was to be one of the last speakers of the four-day seminar. As we all know I would have to be at my best performance because the other speakers who had spoken before me were firstly, more experienced than I was and of course much older than me. They have already spoken except me.

I knew that I was to perform at a level these guys had reached and to cut a long story short; I felt I had done a good job that evening. God blessed these men with awesome revelation and knowledge that eventually led us to a deep discussion after the meeting as I had just opened Pandora's Box. I wished I hadn't opened the box but I had.

I spoke on accepting the full benefits of the death, burial, and resurrection of Jesus, with women in view being made equal to men in many areas of rights and privileges' as one of my key topics.

The temperature was unbearable. It was so sticky and humid that it was important to carefully watch the amount of liquid intake and to consume as much fluid as possible (on a daily basis). In weather like that, dehydration can easily occur if not enough fluid is consumed. The sweat on my forehead was pouring down and I had a tremendous excuse as to why I was perspiring: its summer and everyone should perspire. In reality, it was because of my nervousness in trying so hard to answer hard and deep questions regarding the truth about women's freedom and the right to have a say in whatever part of the world they live in. After my teaching ended, these men were throwing hard questions at me to which I was only able to successfully answer a couple. I thought I had it covered. I thought I knew it all, but it was then that I knew how much truth has yet to be understood and explained. It was the focal point to my search for more understanding of this particular topic and as I invested more time into it, God was faithful to pour more understanding back to me.

Years passed by and God has added to the knowledge about the woman of our day having a say in the Church and in the World. God's awesome grace has enabled me to write and compile this information about such a controversial topic in the Body of Christ, to bring understanding and clarity to the church, and for once and for all, bring some sense to what does not make sense in some very contradictory Biblical writings. Sit back and enjoy!

CHAPTER ONE

Woman's Current World Issues

For centuries, the issue about women not having a say has penetrated deep into the very core of our society in whatever part of the world we live in. This is not something that just happens naturally; it is something that is enforced by a belief, knowledge, or ideas that become converted into tradition that humans observe and pass down from one generation to the next, one nation to another, one race to another, and especially from one church circle to another.

The religions of the World and even church circles have preached hard on this subject: that women are recognized as the lower part of the human life, and that men are the more significant part and should be highly esteemed and served by women in every way. In most societies, women still get lower paying jobs (and are paid with a lower salary rate in regard to having equal jobs), even though their qualifications and ability far exceeds that of men in their company.

In some cultures, they are so ill treated that they are considered a door mat, a sex object, and someone without a say, slaving themselves to their husbands in every way, being in total submission to everything. In the Nation of Ghana Africa, Women are expected and required to have babies. To be a woman barren of having children means that she is good for nothing and totally degraded by the husband, family and the society.

Many other African Nations and, yes, other Nations of the World see a woman's only role as producing babies. In some parts of the World, we see men walking at least a meter ahead of their wives, which depicts the message that women are second-class citizens. This wasn't anything taught as a rule of living, but through the treatment of women, the daily interactions lived out by its society is leaving a psychological influence in the minds of the women. An influence far dangerous than nuclear bombs!

An indirect message that is given to the women through everyday living interactions, behavior at home, in the public and in the religious and cultural world is that they are simply second or third class citizens. Some countries still forbid women the right to vote. In America, the women didn't have this freedom until just a little over 80 years ago.

Eighty plus years prior to the nineteenth amendment, the first serious proposal for women's right to vote in the United States was held at a meeting in Seneca Falls Women's Right Convention. Even in America, one of the countries of the World who claim to be democratic is not too far away from the actual application of equal rights for voting amongst women. Even in America is the issue of discrimination against the sexes a big deal and even now the poison left by its sting is felt almost in every walk of life.

I submit to you, the reader that the most inspiration for this belief comes from the Bible itself. Strange but yes, it's true! Paul was probably referring to Genesis 3:17 when he wrote his letter to Timothy as recorded in I Timothy 2: 12-14, that a woman ought to be silent because the woman is the one tempted and not the man. Cultures, races, and religions, may be in some way directly or indirectly connected to the influence that God's Word (Bible) has provided, but what is so sad is that the influence has not only brought positive results, but also negative and damaging results.

How can that be? Is the Bible divided? Is there an explanation as to why some of the writings in the Bible are so contradictory, so confusing and misleading that even Christian leaders have a hard time explaining? Well, this is a "No Go Zone". What I mean by this is that Pastors would avoid speaking from certain areas of the Bible or verses of Scripture simply because firstly, it's hard to understand, and secondly, difficult to attempt to explain them. Or the ones that have tried will drive us crazy by what they bring to the table as the explanation of them does not make any sense, therefore resulting in legalism and bondage. Christian believers skip reading them just to go to the other ones, and the Church is left with an area in the Body of Christ that the Light of Jesus hasn't fully shone in on it yet. God is a God of revelation and He will not leave us in mystery zone, confused and hanging in limbo. God is moving by His Spirit, bringing the light of the revelation of the Word of God to His Body where we should no longer live mystery.

PSALMS 119: 130 – The unfolding of His Word brings light and it imparts understanding to the simple.

This is God's desire for His people, that they receive the revelation of His Word, imparting understanding and bringing them out of the mystery zone.

In the course of this book, I will attend to a particular "No Go Zone": the issue about the complete freedom that Jesus Christ has brought to the women of our day. I will attempt to bring some sense to these verses because the Bible does make sense. The days we live in are days of revelation and not mystery. The closer we get to the coming of Jesus Christ, the clearer the Scripture will become.

This has been a journey of progressive revelation to the Body of Christ that started after the Ascension of Jesus and the Descending of the Holy Spirit. Everyday toward the "end of days" will get brighter and brighter and our walk and relationship with God should progress according to the progressiveness of the revelation. Mystery days are over!

Why is it that Paul should use statements that would sound so blunt in the Scripture? Where does the Cross of Christ come in to make a difference in this area? Or does it? Please read on because I will answer all these questions and more. Together we will study, explore, and check the validity of each portion of the Scripture and bring some sense to the word and with a sincere heart usher in the freedom that Jesus Christ paid for with his own blood.

PURPOSE OF BOOK

FREEDOM - The purpose for this book is to show and of course bring about the complete freedom Jesus died for to the women of our day, and to set them free from the oppression that has weighed heavily upon them since the fall of man. Religious, cultural, and racial traditions have added more weight upon that already laden burden, and women have struggled to find ways of freedom over the years, both in negative and positive ways. Jesus Christ died a painful death not so we can remain in bondage. No! He's gone through hell so we can enjoy freedom. (It is for freedom that Christ has set you free Galatians 5:1).

TOOLS – The second reason for this book is to provide the tools needed for pastors and leaders to answer questions that are often unanswered. Confused members of the Body of Christ, namely the women, stand divided internally whether to do what their hearts crave for, to be that significant someone that God has created them to be, or to settle with the "God saying shut up, sit down, don't try to lead" belief that has dominated the church of God in the past centuries. There are numerous women in this day and age who have broken free from these traditions and are used by God today as instruments of great blessings, both to the world as a whole and to the Body of Christ.

The free ones are in a huge minority. Imagine the countless women in the majority bound up by cultures, races, religion and ideas. Change will happen, and it will begin with leaders who take the time to train and equip them in this particular area, and you are doing just that if you are reading this book right now. It is my desire and prayers to God that this book will make a difference in your life and give you a clearer and a more sound doctrine for the edification of the Body of Christ.

CHAPTER TWO
Understanding Traditions

"EVERYTHING IS PERMISSIBLE BUT NOT EVERYTHING IS BENEFICIAL".

This is a quote of the Apostle Paul, and I do think that it would benefit us a lot if we hold to it as a principle of life, because it would help us to perceive and embrace the things we encounter in life in a filtering manner. Filtering manner of life is to run a check on everything that comes our way, checking the value thereof. Sometimes we cancel theories, things and issues too prematurely, and we don't really give enough time to the investigation of an issue.

Ecclesiastes 7: 25a I applied my heart to know, to search and seek out wisdom and the reason of things, NKJV.

Putting that sentence in modern day language is to say; "why we do what we do."

If we use that as a rule for living our lives, we will definitely go back and attempt to restore, reinvent or revive that which we have cancelled prematurely because we have come to realize how valuable they are. If it only draws life out of you, drop it; it is not worth holding on to. But if it adds to you, bringing some sort of benefit to your life, then it is definitely worth holding on to. We would be sure to save marriages, families, and even our Christian walk if we would operate by that principle.

In this book, we will be using this principle as a knife to slice open traditions; particularly the traditions about the women of our day that I happen to believe have been deprived of their equal rights and positions as women of God. Dear reader, you are urged to read and study with sincerity as I build the foundation for our teaching, keeping an open mind and allowing yourself not only to study and learn, but also to soak into the truth of God's Word and be transformed by the renewing of your mind.

WHAT IS TRADITION?

Tradition according to Webster's New World Dictionary is "the handing down orally of beliefs, customs etc"

In light of the New Testament, these are words used to describe traditions: observance, rules and regulations, and ordinances. At some point, traditions are also described as "wisdom of men." The children of Israel were given ordinances, rules, and regulations to observe, preserve, and pass down from one generation to the next as tradition. To observe them still after Jesus Christ's death is regarded by Paul as a manifestation of human wisdom.

God gave these traditions to the Israelites to observe, but when Jesus came and died on the cross, they still had their meaning but they had lost the power. They can be observed as a custom, but we cannot bank on its power; they have lost their sacredness immediately after the death of Jesus Christ. In the Scripture, they are said to be a shadow and not the real thing.

Of course, they had all the power invested in it for use under the old covenant, but when the real thing has come (Jesus), they are no longer of any use to the children of Israel. They have been stripped off its power because every one of those religious ceremony, observance or tradition only acts as a symbol of Jesus Christ who is the real thing.

Hebrews 10:1- The law is only a shadow of the good things that are coming, not the realities themselves.

Shadows are not the real thing, but they sure describe what the real thing would portray. Just looking at the shadow of a hand tells us that it is a hand of a person. In the Old Testament, the sacrificial Blood of bulls and goats which were used as a form of cleansing from sin and the atonement thereof represents the blood of Jesus. It is used by the Children of Israel to wash and clean them up externally, whereas the blood of Jesus cleanses Christians internally from their sin and guilt conscience of the heart. The author of Hebrews shares some of this great insight in his Letters and they provide affirmations to what we are saying.

HEBREWS 9: 13 – The Blood of Goats and Bulls and the ashes of Heifer sprinkled on those who are ceremonially unclean sanctify them so that they are outwardly clean.

Notice this verse promises the provision for external cleansing by the sacrificial blood of Bulls and Goats and in verse 14, it gives us the reality it symbolizes.

HEBREWS 9: 14-How much more, then will the Blood of Christ, who through the eternal Spirit offered Himself unblemished to God, cleanse our conscience from acts that lead to death, so that we may serve the Living God!

Over in verse 14, the Blood of Jesus washes and cleanses internally. It reaches what Old Covenant Sacrifices cannot reach, the heart, the spiritual and atones also for its Sin, preparing the individual person to serve from the heart without a guilty conscience.

HEBREWS 10: 22- let us draw near to God with a sincere heart in full assurance of faith, having our hearts sprinkled to cleanse us from a guilty conscience and having our bodies washed with pure water.

Better than the Old Covenant sacrifices the Blood of Jesus the Son of God, cleanses not only our hearts but our bodies too. Praise God in the Highest!

The Israelites are still observing the shadow of the real thing, and if they choose to do so I say why not? I think God would want for them, as a Nation to keep their culture just like He would want for the Nations of the World to keep theirs as long as its principles are beneficial. If the principles behind a culture are demonic, then one ought to seriously consider reshuffling or even dropping them depending on the nature of its content.

Any culture that has a good meaning for life or Godliness needs preservation, but anything that has the slightest sign of demonic involvement, witchcraft, immorality or just the demeaning of the human species needs to be abandoned! The demeaning of the human species denotes the idea of gender inequality, age inequality or (color) racial inequality.

We, however, the Christian society have a culture, some of it may need reshuffling, and some of it needs total abandonment as long as it takes away and does not add value to our Christian, and individual values. A culture, again, can be a good thing or a bad thing, and then it becomes traditional, passed down from one generation to the next. My question to you before we proceed, do you have a culture, and is it healthy and good that needs preservation or do you need to abandon it because of the ugliness it carries? Some religious beliefs are as ugly as Hell!

CHAPTER THREE
The New Order

HEBREWS 9: 10 –Concerned only with foods and drinks, various washings, and fleshly ordinances imposed until the time of reformation.

The second part of that verse states "ordinances imposed until the time of reformation," tells us that all blessings, all rules and regulations has come to the end because Jesus, the one who will bring the New Order of things has come. God did impose these ordinances upon the Children of Israel, but only to lead up to the coming of Jesus in human form that has taken place over two thousand years ago.

He has come as a man and died rose and is alive today with the New Order already in force. These external regulations are only applied until the time of the New Order. The New Order begins at the death, burial and resurrection of Jesus. Let us understand that the laws are external and physical, whereas the New Order is internal and spiritual.

COLOSSIANS 2: 16-17-So let no one judge you with foods and drinks, or regarding a festival or a New Moon or Sabbath, which are a shadow of things to come, but the substance is of Christ.

The result of the new order is found in Colossians 2: 16-17. Paul states that the old order is no longer needed as a measuring standard for the Body or even the Children of Israel since it is only a shadow of the real thing, and the real thing is Christ. Finding ourselves in a place of eating meats that were forbidden by God under the old covenant should not lead us to condemning ourselves or even letting others condemn us because the power and sacredness behind this ritual has been done away with.

To eat those foods does not make one to sin. Yet it does have some hygiene points behind them, and I do think we should pay attention to them, for which there has to be a level of caution and moderation when approaching these foods and drinks, but the primary symbolic meaning it stands for is done away with. An example is; why did God forbid the Israelites from eating pork?

Pigs feed from basically what is dirt or garbage. To prevent oneself from indulging in pork would be regarded as observing holiness through restraining the flesh from such craving. This however is symbolic to saying No to the carnal cravings of the flesh that we all possess as human beings concerning the filth of the World. Just to name a few of them would be immoralities, pornography, stealing, lying and cheating, etc, etc.

To see people still trying to observe these religious rituals or traditions doesn't mean that it has some form of holiness or power. NO! All there is - a form of religious duties without the power. It is empty and void with power. It is just a shadow. It's like holding a pistol filled with blanks where it makes a noise, it even has sparks at the end of the barrel, but it does not hit the target nor does it make an impact. Any organization or religious movement that observes these O.T. ordinances must know that there is nothing to it that's sacred, just a form of Godliness denying the true power.

Let's study the shadow side converted to reality. I've only picked some to use as examples. Those on the shadow side or what it stands for in the Old Testament are on one side and the real thing on the other. The first table shows names representing the two Covenants:

These are only applied till the time of the New Order

(Hebrews- 9: 9-10).

OLD TESTAMENT	NEW TESTAMENT
OLD ORDER	NEW ORDER
EXTERNAL	INTERNAL
PHYSICAL	SPIRITUAL
SHADOWS	REALITIES

The second table shows the shadow converted to reality:

1 Circumcision of the flesh Colossians 2: 11	Circumcision of the heart Romans 2: 29
2 Foods and drinks/ ceremonial washings. External procedures. Hebrews 9: 9- 10, Mark 7: 1-23	Sanctification from sin is reality of the ceremonial washings.
3 Blood of Bulls and Goats atoning for the sins of Israel. Hebrews 9: 13	Blood of Jesus to atone for our sins. Hebrews 9: 14
4 Worldly tabernacle/ Copy of the real thing. Hebrews 8: 3- 5	The Heavenly tabernacle that Christ entered. Hebrews 8: 1- 2

Those are just some examples of the shadow and the real thing, external and internal, the physical and the spiritual. In the words of Jesus himself, He confirmed this fact in:

John 3-12 when he said; "I have spoken of earthly things and you do not believe; how then will you believe if I speak of heavenly things."

Jesus was basically using earthly matters to communicate spiritual messages. God had to speak in our level of understanding and earthliness. We as human beings find it difficult to understand spiritual matters if He were to communicate to us with spiritual things because the Spirit has not been given yet, Christ has not died.

After His death, the Spirit has come. Along with the blessed Holy Spirit, spiritual matters are brought to our understanding by the revelation of the Spirit. The Holy Spirit in us quickens our minds to conceive and perceive, to understand spiritual things, to differentiate the shadow from the real things, and to know the very meaning of the Scriptures. Once we've gotten hold of the real things, it is then high time to let go of the shadow, not the real things!

Rules and regulations have been observed as traditions by the children of Israel, where it was acting as shadows of the real thing. As Christians of the 21st century, we do not have a problem with many of those traditions, but we definitely have problems with how we treat the women of our day, both in Churches and the World at large. In the course of this study we will focus our energy into slicing open not only traditions but also ideas, checking for value and validity. We will then hold onto those ones that add value, beneficial, and are still valid to this day.

The ultimate question we should begin to ask ourselves is whether it is still valid or has it expired without our knowledge?

CHAPTER FOUR

Understanding the Time

One of the existing problems today in the area of Bible doctrine is failure to understand the different time periods spoken of in the Bible. Avoiding the loopholes, we must understand the two major time periods, which are as follows: before the death, burial and resurrection of Jesus, and after the death, burial, and resurrection of Jesus. Misinterpretation of the scripture may have also been the result of misunderstanding the Bible times and periods.

According to the Pauline Epistles (letters written by Paul) the two time periods he talked about were the past and the future, and that basically is the same two time periods, which were the before- death and the after-resurrection time periods. From a Biblical point of view, the past is all the way from Genesis to Jesus' death, burial and ends with resurrection, but the future begins with the resurrection all the way to the making new of all things or the New Kingdom that God will set up in the near future. The future according to the Epistles is also categorized in a time known as the days of the "dispensation of Grace".

So have a picture in your minds, the two Bible time periods. The past is all the way from Genesis to the death, burial and resurrection of Jesus. The future, also known as the time of the dispensation of Grace, is the time we are living in right now. We are in the future that began from the resurrection of Jesus, all the way to the making new of all things by Almighty God. We are in the very middle of this dispensation of Grace, and it hasn't ended yet! It is absolutely fantastic to live in the greatest moment in human history whereby Grace is so randomly dispensed. The future is now!

The Disciples of Jesus, Paul and other men and women of God were the very first ones to enjoy the dispensation of this Grace. It began with them but it does not end with them. Grace is still dispensed, distributed freely and to everyone who is willing to receive. Awesome Grace is available to the Body of Christ today!

This Grace enables us as members of the Body of Jesus to understand and administer the Grace of God in relation to our gifts and office. God has placed us in different offices of ministry and has given us gifts and Grace pertaining to them. This Grace "dispensed", acts as the enabler in performing the duties that we as individuals have been assigned with. We become more like "Naturals" in our area of gifting.

Paul, a teacher of the Bible, the man by revelation authored almost half of the New Testament, whose teachings stand today as foundation principles for the Church of Jesus Christ, admits that there are other prophets and Holy men of God who have been dispensed with Grace unto revelation just like him. He reveals the fact that Grace is freely dispensed today to His Church.

Ephesians 3:2-5 If you have heard of the dispensation of the Grace of God, which is given me to you ward: How that by revelation he made known unto me the mystery: (as I wrote afore in few words). Whereby when ye read, ye may understand my Knowledge in mystery of Christ. Which in other ages was not made known unto the sons of men, as it is now revealed unto his Holy Prophets and Apostles by his Spirit.

Verses 2 through 4 speak of Paul talking about the dispensed Grace upon his life that enabled him to understand the mystery of Christ through revelation, to grasp the full meaning of Christ's entire mission, death, burial, and resurrection and the benefits that would follow. Paul was the one who paved the way for Christianity to where it is today in the light of the correct knowledge of God.

His letters are the detailed teachings of what God did through His son Jesus Christ. If we desire what is rightfully ours as Christians, let us not go to the Old Testament or the Gospels but begin to go to the Epistles for a clear answer.

The Old Testament and the Gospels are great and important. They are still valid up to this very day. But our true identity, our rightful inheritance, our Christian walk are all found in the Epistles with great clarity and simplicity.

Our problem today is that we invest far too much time in the Old Testament, spending far too much time preaching from the Old Testament and the Gospels rather than the Epistles. As it is known, "The Old Testament is the New Testament revealed, and the New Testament is the Old Testament concealed", why go to the concealed (Old Testament) when it has been revealed to us with great clarity through Holy men who have taken the time to write them? However, important to note that the Spirit is the revealer!

The Old Testament is like a wild ox still running wild. The Gospels are like ox already butchered and stored away in the refrigerator as meat. But the Epistles are like meat cooked with special ingredients, ready to be served. Notice the breaking down of the process to the point it becomes not just delicious but edible. That is the Epistles for us, delicious and edible. It is okay to read study and preach from the Old Testament or the Gospels, but one has to be familiar with the two time periods, the two Orders and the dispensation of Grace which will all be found in the Epistles. One has to be familiar with the New Testament theology.

The Epistles contain the real thing. Every little detail of Jesus coming to earth, His death, burial and resurrection are in the Epistles. Everything regarding the Christian position and rights, the Christian Worship, the Christian lifestyle and off course the Christian service are all detailed in it. Where else can we look for a greater understanding of God things, but the Epistles of Paul and other letters too?

Paul admitted that there would be other men and women of God who would also be dispensed Grace to allow them to see things they did not personally see or understand.

A Closer Look at Ephesians 3: 5; tells us that Paul wasn't the only one that God was dispensing this Grace but other men and women of God too, both in his time and the future also. What is my point? Paul with all the revelation and knowledge given to him, that he comes up with almost half the New Testament, he never claimed to be the only one. He admitted that there would be other men and women of God who would also be dispensed Grace to allow them to see things he did not personally see or understand.

Why wouldn't God give all the knowledge to just one person? There is so much that God wants to give humanity. One person only cannot handle the depth of the revelation of the knowledge of the Word of God. Revelation of God's word is deep and it requires time and people for its full comprehension. This is a progressive occasion, the revelation of the Word of God in and through human intellectual ability. It cannot be attained in one incident or in one lifetime.

Ephesians 3- 5: Which in other ages was not made known unto the sons of men, as it is now revealed unto his Holy Apostles and Prophets by the Spirit;

Notice the word "now". It is speaking of any day after the resurrection of Jesus Christ and the Holy Spirit being sent down to Earth. It is a particular time that begins from the resurrection of Jesus all the way to the present day and continues on into the future, all the way to the making new of all things (The renovation of the earth and the eternal reign of the Son of God). This time period (Now), is also known to be the "dispensation of Grace", the very reason Paul was talking about the dispensation of this Grace not only to him but to many other people as well.

We are still in the "Now" period, the dispensation of Grace where everything to make your life more heavenly, more blessed, more fulfilled and much better has already been paid for by the blood of Jesus and is freely dispensed today to you and for you, the Body of Christ.

One other thing I'd like to point out is that Grace is also dispensed to His Holy **Prophets and Apostles**. "Plural", not singular, which then confirms the fact that Paul, is not the only inspired, to bring about the revelation of the mystery. There are many others called including some in this day and age. We have more books written today by men and women for the one purpose of bringing clarity to those things in the Word that once were a mystery.

From a Biblical standpoint and view of time, the past other ages that Paul was talking about begins from Genesis to the death and burial of Jesus but "now" begins in the resurrection. Let me explain my case as to why I believe the "now" time begins with the resurrection and not Jesus' death or burial.

After Jesus arose from the dead, he let himself be seen by Mary Magdalene. Mary wanted to reach out and touch the Lord, but the Lord Jesus told her not to touch him. (John 20:16-17)

I have wondered for a great many years why Jesus would not allow Mary to touch him.

Jesus responded to Mary and said; "Do not touch me for I have not been to the Father yet". Pay attention to the key phrase **"have not been to the Father yet"** and keep your thoughts along those lines. Hebrews 9:12-gives a startling connection to the meaning of the words of Jesus during the time He spoke these words to Mary.

Hebrews 9:12 Neither by the blood of Goats and Calves, but by His own blood He entered in once into the Holy Place; having obtained eternal redemption for us.

Notice the part that says **"by His own blood He entered in once into the Holy Place"** to obtain eternal redemption. After his resurrection from the dead, He was to appear before the throne of His Father once, the first and the only time He was going to present His own blood as an evidence that He really did die, shed his blood for the sole purpose that His blood would serve as a price to fully obtain our redemption that is available eternally.

When He spoke those words to Mary, He was actually saying: "Don't touch me Mary." We don't want to temper with the evidence or to do anything to contaminate it. I'd like to preserve this evidence for the highest court as proof to my Father that it's paid in full. Thank God He did just that! Free at last! Free at last! Oh how they've been freed at last!"

Drawing my own conclusion, this is probably the last of Jesus' temptation to abort His mission. I thank God for His Son who would not allow any form of temptation to sabotage His mission in His final steps to Victory, because He had our freedom and of course the freedom of all women in His mind. This begun not when He died or when He was buried, but when He arose and came into the throne room of the Father to obtain eternal salvation.

The "now" period begins on the day of resurrection which makes the days we live in the 'now' period, the period in which Grace is so much available and is so much dispensed randomly to everybody who may be willing, especially to the Body of Christ.

I just don't get it. The church has become so mean, preaching legalism, preaching about a God who is just about to slay you the minute you make your next mistake, a wrathful God, slam bang mean machine. Christians threaten one another quoting from particular Scriptures assuming that this type of disciplinc is a God thing and that people's lives would be straightened out if all they hear were harsh words. How can that possibly be when the days we live in are known to be the dispensation of Grace?

I was in Fiji the month of December 2008 teaching for a solid two months in a Church my brother-in-law is the pastor. During those meetings I kept hearing one of the leaders saying; "let's be careful or the Lord will hate us." Where in the World did the Church get all these types of theology? It's a wacky theology! It is no wonder why the World thinks the Church is half crank, wacky and weird!

God is not trying to kick us out of heaven; he is trying to get everybody into His beautiful Heaven. He's not trying to take good things away from us; He's trying to give us something better. Do I disagree with the wrath of God? Absolutely not! But I don't agree with believing that every bad thing happening in this world right now is a manifestation of the wrath of God, because it's not.

Romans 2:4 tells us that God's forbearance, longsuffering, and goodness leads people to repentance, and in verse 5 it tells us that His wrath is stored away for judgment day. Today and now, what we see around is not His wrath yet, but what is, is longsuffering and goodness because it is the Grace period. It is not the day of wrath yet. Verse 5 tells us that there is a day of wrath and judgment where His righteous judgment will be revealed. That day is coming and you can be sure that it's going to be a just judgment of all humankind, but that day is not yet and is definitely not today!

Again let me say this, God uses His goodness to bring people to repentance and wrath is only for judgment. The point is: in this dispensation of Grace which is right now, today, whatever today means for you, you and I are the talked about candidates in Ephesians 3:1-5 as recipients to that greatly dispensed Grace. Since we are in the "now" period we are the people been given Grace and very much of it.

We have all received from the fullness of Him, Grace upon Grace. John 1:16

For the Law came through Moses but Grace and Truth came through Jesus Christ. John 1:17

Under the Law, the High Priest who would attend to the Holiest of all has a rope tied to his ankles, and bells that are hanging from his Robe would sound and cling when he moves around to perform his priestly duties. If there were no sound for a while then the other priests would know that he is down (dead) for whatever reason. The other priests who were outside wouldn't dare go inside for fear of death so they will then pull on the rope to bring the dead priest out.

The Old Testament was a scary Covenant to embrace because it carries a heavier responsibility if treated lightly, it would invite the Wrath of God. When Jesus died, the veil of the sanctuary was torn from top to bottom signifying that everyone can enter into the Holiest of all without fear but with boldness. The fear of being slain by a just God has dissolved because the Covenant is a better covenant, one of Grace and truth.

As I have said earlier, from a Biblical standpoint and view of time, the past other ages, begins from Genesis to resurrection. The period from resurrection till today all falls in the category of the "now". How do we see Bible time? It is before the Spirit time and during the Spirit time, the legalistic time of the law and the time of the dispensation of Grace, therefore we are still in the same 'now' Paul spoke about, which is the Spirit and Grace dispensation period. I said all that to prepare you the reader, for what is coming in our future chapters. I am building the foundation for my case in regard to our common subject: "the freedom of all women".

CHAPTER FIVE

Complete Revelation and Partial Understanding

What I am about to say in this chapter will shock some of you and even offend some of you to the point of throwing this book away and not reading it. Don't make that mistake because you'll miss the complete truth behind this theory. Paul, the man who was given the complete revelation about the works of the cross of Jesus Christ, must have understood what was revealed to him only partially. I believe this to be true. In His letter to the church in Galatians 3:28, he said that there is no longer a separation between a male and a female. This gives complete contradiction to the things he said in his letter to Timothy.

I Timothy 2:12 - I suffer not a woman teach in the Churches nor try to usurp authority over the man.

Notice the contradiction. He believed in a sense of the revelation given him that the woman has as much access as the man. But in other letters he writes to other people, he reveals that the woman still doesn't have access to many privileges. What's the deal here?

He received a complete revelation about the works of the Cross of Jesus making the two parties, male and female, become one, but the light of that revelation knowledge only shone partially to his understanding. His understanding of its application to the lives of the women was only partial.

He wasn't able to see its complete application because of the former knowledge about the women of his culture. The knowledge that acts as a restraint, and that limits women from many different access. His partial understanding is due to his boxed-in culture, the environment of his exposure, and the unexplained knowledge of the Holy Spirit. No doubt Paul had a special call. No doubt he received a complete revelation that indicates the flawlessness of the whole Bible. It is however, the finite ability in the recipient that caused him to only see the applications partially. I will reveal more on this in later chapters.

Progressive nature of Revelation

What do I mean by the unexplained knowledge of the Holy Spirit?

The Holy Spirit was not able to give all the knowledge to one person all at one time because one individual cannot handle the depth of God's wisdom and understanding. That's the reason Paul made mention of other Holy men and Prophets of this Grace period, also recipients of Knowledge.

Revelation is progressive in nature. It takes more than one person and a great deal of time. I'd say that we who live in this day have more spiritual knowledge than those in the early days of the Church. The farther away we are from resurrection day the more understanding of knowledge we will beget and conceive. Over the years the Church has been building on one revelation after another.

The revelation that comes now upon the Church does not mean deletion or addition to the whole Bible. The progressive revelation of today is the revelation of understanding the applications of the revelation (Bible).

The Church is much better today in knowledge than when it first started around two thousand plus years ago. How is that? Well, ponder on the thoughts of this scripture for a while.

Ephesians 5: 27- That He might present it to Himself a Glorious Church, not having spot or wrinkle, or any such thing; but that it should be Holy and without blemish.

The above verse speaks of the plan of God for the Church at the end of the age, the end result for the Church. God will work on His Church so that it will go from Glory to Glory and more Glory. By the time He presents the Church to Himself, it would be up to the standard expected, Glorious Church!

That is His purpose and the means to bring the purpose to pass is in verse 26; which speaks of the washing of the water by the Word of God. The knowledge of the Word of God prepares the Church for what's coming, the Glory of God. The billions of Christian literature today is a sign that the Church has progressed further toward where it should be, Glorious Church.

Let's look at this connection for a moment.

Numbers 14: 20, 21, 22, 23 The Lord replied, "I have forgiven them, as you asked. Nevertheless, as surely as I live and as surely as the Glory of the Lord fills the whole Earth, not one of the men who saw my Glory and the miraculous signs I performed in Egypt and in the desert but who disobeyed me and tested me ten times- not one of them will see the land I promised on oath to their forefathers.

In these verses, God made a sure promise that the ones who saw His miracles in the desert will not enter into the Promised Land, and assured them that this promise is as sure as the Glory of the Lord fills the Earth. I propose to you that the Glory of the Lord has already filled the whole Earth at this time, and as sure as that is, so shall the promise of God to the Israel to not go into the promise land but to perish in the desert. In short, the whole earth is full of Gods glory, even now.

Isaiah 6: 3 – the earth is full of His Glory.

Isaiah states the same thing. The whole Earth is full of His Glory but not the people, not the Church yet. This Glory has yet to fill the Church.

This next passage deserves a little extra attention because theological Christian beliefs have been built upon this verse alone and has the church as a whole almost like a limping and wounded warrior. Common sense tells us that the limping wounded warrior will eventually die; it's just a matter of time. It's been limping not because of flaw within the scripture but within the people bringing the translation. This scripture has been misinterpreted for at least over a century due to taking scripture out of its context and building a doctrine from it. Take a look at this portion of scripture for a moment. What do you think it means? If your answer is that you are a sinner even though you're a born again Christian, than you are a victim of religious heresy.

Romans 3: 23 – for all have sinned and fall short of the Glory.

Paul makes mention how we **all** fall short of the Glory because of sin. The first thing we need to establish is who does the **"all"** Paul refers to in the above scripture. Paul is referring to two major parties, Jews and Gentiles, who encompassed the whole World.

Romans 3: 9-What then? Are we better than they? Not at all! For we have previously charged both Jews and Greeks *that they are* all *under sin.*

Paul being a Jew asks this question as to whether they (the Jews) are better than the Gentiles. He answers his own question by saying that the Jews were no better than the Gentiles and how both parties are equally under sin. The both parties mentioned here are Jews and Gentiles. The Jews are a small group of people and the Gentiles are every race and tribe in this World. **The Jews and Gentiles consist of the whole World, which in short, "all" according to the words of the author.**

The ultimate truth is that every human being on planet Earth is born a sinner. Born with sin nature in his or her members and most of all in their human spirits! Romans 3:23 reveals that every one of us have fallen short of the Glory of God because every one of us have sinned and have the sin nature in ourselves. We, including the Jews, are categorized as sinners as long as we are born of woman.

From verses 10- 20speaks of the hopeless and helpless situation of sin both Jews and Gentile are in. Paul refers to them as "all", and that no, not one is righteous. Sin of all kind was revealed by the author in this passage to be found within the children of the World, Jews and Gentiles, the "all" he was referring to. There is totally nothing good in humanity. No one, no, not one is justified righteous in the sight of God, for all are locked up in sin's penitentiary, both Jews and Gentiles.

But we have good news coming right along in verse 21 where Paul begins with a conjunction, "but." But speaks a great deal of how the whole message unfolds, it brings a new twist into the story, it brings the good news to all the world, that there is hope for their sinful, helpless and hopeless state. The question we are to ask is; "what is the hope and when?" How is this hope available? Let us look to the next verse for the answer.

Verses 21- 23 are jumbled up where they are not in their correct sequence and therefore the sincere bible reader wouldn't be able to understand. Let's further exegete this passage for clarity. After establishing that both Jews and Gentiles alike are under sin; the **"all"** Paul was referring to, important to note that both their need is righteousness. Every human beings special need is to be righteous again. The law couldn't make them righteous so a righteousness from God has come through faith in Christ to **"all"** who believe whether Jew or Gentile because **"all"** have sinned and fall short of the Glory of God.

Romans 3: 23 only reveal our state of sinfulness before Christ. A place both Jews and Gentiles stand in before Christ. This righteousness has come to both (all) because they are sinners and need it. But once the righteousness has come to them and they accept it, they cease to be sinners but the righteousness of God in Christ.

Obviously, this righteousness will come to those who will receive Jesus in his/her heart. Jesus is the righteousness of God therefore to receive Him is to receive righteousness. I do not consider myself a sinner anymore but the righteousness of God in Christ. Let us observe once more key words of verse 22:

This righteousness from God comes through Faith in Jesus Christ to all who believe (Rom 3: 22). NIV

Get the picture; it came from God, through Jesus the bridge, and then to all who believe, destination. God gave it, Jesus delivered it, and I received it when I received Jesus, the righteousness of God.

II Corinthians 5:21- For He (Father God) made Him (Jesus) who had no sin to be sin for us, so that we (you & me) might become the righteousness of God in Him.

That scripture is truly a scripture foundation for true believers identity because it has stated a done work, a done deal in Calvary where Jesus became us and we became Him. It's a done deal where our new identity is that we are righteous, the great exchange.

Now, if those scriptures and its explanations have not convinced you enough that you are the righteous, then how about this next one.

Romans 5:19-For as through the one man's disobedience the many are made sinners, even so the obedience of the One the many will be made righteous.

The first one man who disobeyed was the first Adam, and as a result many (you and me) are made sinners. Therefore the second one man, who is Jesus (Last Adam), became obedient and as a result the many were made righteous. Every one of us stood in the affecting ripple of the first Adam.

The ripple effect of the Choice of the First Adam does not require your choice. The affecting ripple effect of the last Adam does require your choice.

Man's sinful state does not involve any choice from them at all; they were born in the rippling effects of the sin of the first Adam. However, to be adopted into the family of the Last Adam, to experience the effects of His obedience and be made righteous is a choice we all will have to make. I know what it is to stand in both of the family line. I am still standing in one and that is the lineage of the last Adam. When I made the choice to accept the righteousness of God (Jesus), I was transferred from being a sinner to being the righteousness of God in Christ.

Romans 8: 10 – But if Christ is in you, your body is dead because of sin; yet your spirit is alive because of righteousness. (NIV Bible)

When we accept Christ, He then lives in us. The above scripture tells us that our body is dead because of sin. How is that so? Well, to accept Jesus is to accept what He has done, as if we ourselves did that entire work He did. His victories become our victories, Praise God! When he condemned sin in His own body on the cross, He was actually taking your place of death to sin and victory over that wretched body of sin, which leads you astray into temptation.

To accept Him is to accept your reality which is the New you in Christ. Also righteousness like a parcel is placed in our spirits, who is Jesus the Son of the Living God. Now then, we have a responsibility to live according to the righteousness of God in us, and not the human nature in our members that has already been put to death.

If that does not convince you either that you are the righteousness of God in Christ and not a sinner, I don't know what will!

I conclude that the state of a person as a sinner was the old him/her until righteousness comes to him/her, whether Jew or Gentile. In saying that this righteousness is now come to "all", indicates that both Jews and Gentiles alike are in true need for righteousness.

Furthering my conclusion is that this phrase here in verse 23 is not a permanent position of humans whether Jew or Gentile but a position of being a qualified candidate to receive the righteousness of God and be made one. A state every human being was in before accepting Jesus as Savior and Lord. But whoever has accepted this righteousness has become one.

From our previous pages, we have asked the question as to whom, how and when the Church will be filled with the Glory of God.

First, the whole Earth is filled with the Glory of God. According to the book of Romans 1: 20; the whole Earth has clearly revealed to all Humanity the Glory of the invincible God. Psalm 19:1 says that the Heavens reveal the Glory of God. It has covered the whole Earth.

Secondly, the people of the Earth are not all filled with the Glory because not all have received the righteousness of God yet. Those who have not accepted the righteous package, "Jesus Christ" are not in any way, shape or form to qualify for the Glory of God.

Do I really believe that? Absolutely! Every fiber of my being believes that. But when one chooses to accept the righteous package (Jesus), he or she is no longer falling short of the Glory of God, rather an access to the Glory.

Colossian 1:27 to whom God willed to make known what is the riches of the Glory of this mystery among the Gentiles, which is Christ in you, the hope of Glory.

We as Christians are not falling short of the Glory. We are filled with the potential of the Glory and are able to live up to what glorifies God because of the fact that Christ is in us. Do Christians fail to live up to that? Do they live in sin at times? Absolutely! And that could be derived from bad choices or a lack of knowledge in the God things. Now notice what Paul mentioned in Colossian 1:27, that Christ in us is not the Glory but the hope to the Glory which is the potential of a glorified life. To accept Christ in our hearts is just potential, access and entry point to the great glory of God.

What is lacking? We know that according to Ephesians 5:27; Christ is returning back to Earth for a Church full of the Glory of Himself. If Christ is just an ingredient to see the Glory of God manifest in our lives, then what would be the next ingredient that would go along with the first ingredient? Look up this verse for a minute:

Habakkuk 2:14-for the whole Earth will be filled with the knowledge of the Glory of God as the waters cover the Sea.

Knowledge is the other ingredient that goes along with Christ in us, in order for us to see the Glory of Christ in us. Whatever we want to receive would need to be received intellectually before we can receive them spiritually and physically. To receive the knowledge of the Glory prepares us to receive the Glory of God.

In summary to the fact that revelation is progressive, and that it has been unfolding for quite a while now since the birth of the Church, the Church is very much full of the Glory since when it was first started. By the time Jesus returns to Earth, the Church will be so full of Glory because the progression of revelation knowledge has paved the way. I happen to believe that the Church is much better today that when it first started, even though the church in many instances have failed.

The setbacks in Church circles happen just to show that we are not perfect. So could this mean that Paul had a partial understanding of the revelation that God was giving him? Absolutely! The man had a complete revelation but a partial understanding. He had some practical understanding applicable for His time and culture but we live in a different time and are exposed to an ever-evolving culture.

With Paul's lack of understanding in this area, am I saying that his teaching should be eradicated from the Bible? Absolutely not! If it weren't for Paul's teaching, we would not be where we are today. I believe that some of Paul's teaching was put in the Bible for this reason, to prepare us for information such as these, where we can better understand some of the most glaring contradictions in the Church. When Paul first mentioned them, they were just blocks to build on and over the centuries, the Church has built upon them.

God giving man a complete revelation depicts the flawlessness of the epistles, but it is fair however, to say that the recipient of the complete revelation is still embodied in frail humanity, complete with human inadequacy and imperfections.

Not one single sentence or line in the Holy Bible is to be replaced. We just have to grow in knowledge and the understanding of it. This is like buying a new computer, complete in everything, but you never got to understand everything about it on the first day. It takes time for you to understand the technicalities of it. It's not the computer but the person that's received it. Paul was the same way where his level of understanding at the time was partial.

CHAPTER SIX

Cultural Evolution

The knowledge was appropriate and fitting for the people because of a lack of understanding the revelations of God. While Paul was writing his letters to Timothy, he had in mind the three related culture of that time and place which was Rome, Israel and Ephesus. Ephesus was dominated by the teaching of a goddess called Diana. The first rule of interpretation is that the author had something in mind that he was writing about.

Joe B. Fuiten, Senior pastor of Cedar Park Assembly of God in Bothel, Washington mentioned this in his book: "The Revenge of Ephesus." Pg 6

"Ephesus was the center of feminism, environmentalism, paganism, the sexual revolution, astrology, and anti Christian fervor."

Joe Fuiten introduced in his book that Paul whilst writing to Timothy, puts the Woman of Ephesus that have been saved, and that are coming in with the baggage of their culture which was a feminist dominated culture in their place of submission. Paul had to make sure that the women who have come into the Church are dealt with appropriately regarding the baggage they are bringing. If what Joe said was so, then there are three cultures that interrelate at one point and they are women either dominated or they are dominating the man. The other two cultures were the Roman culture and the Jewish one.

If the three cultures that Paul was speaking about were the lens that Paul looked through, it would be justifiable at least to say that they were only mandatory at that time. We live in a different time and place. These two aspects need to be taken into consideration, considering the culture of the World has greatly evolved. If taken literally today the way it was written at that time, there will be a sure possibility of wrong doctrines, which we as a Church have experienced ourselves resulting in legalistic rules and bondage. Some of these teachings were there to help us better understand the Bible; the works of Jesus and of course, the understanding of Scripture and clarity of God's will and purpose.

The Words of God is powerful and effective back then as it is for us today. The Word hasn't changed, will never change and must never be changed! The Word has to be accepted although some things need to be reconsidered such as the time it was written, culture of that day, and who were the immediate audience the author was writing to. Also look at the whole context of what is written in the related versus and chapters. We must not try and build on an isolated scripture, nor should we try and build a doctrine out of assumptions. I strongly believe that the scripture must interpret scripture. What this means is that the Word line up with the rest of the scriptures and should make sense.

It was too much for Paul, but it wasn't something he should be blamed for. God used him to receive the complete revelation, and also other men and women of God that were graced with grace to understand fully the revelation. There are many men and women of God in these times that understand fully the revelation than the ones around a hundred years ago. By reading through Roberts Liardon's first of three God's Generals series, the lives of great Men and Women of God that have shaped the World of Christian living.

These Men and Women demonstrated dynamic faith, outstanding boldness and the manifestation of the gifts of the Spirit. There is however, a famine of spiritual knowledge; the inadequate knowledge of the Word of God was obvious through some or even all of them. They knew so little but yet do so much, whereas today the Church as we know it to be, know so much but yet do so little.

Although that is the case, I still am glad to be a recipient of the revealed knowledge of the Word of God that is widely dispensed by the Grace of Jesus and distributed by faithful men. The closer we are to the coming of Jesus, the clearer revelation knowledge will be to the Body of Christ. Revelation and understanding is a progressive matter.

Strong Preparation for Chapters Ahead:

CORRECTING MISINTERPRETATIONS

After concluding with chapter five, we will prepare our minds for what's coming up in the chapters ahead that will deal with the words of the Apostle Paul, word by word.

These texts and words of Paul were either unexplained or misinterpreted, but as we had talked about earlier, the Bible does makes sense and by the help of the Blessed Holy Spirit and his Holy servants of the now, these so-called untouched, unexplained, or misinterpreted areas can now be visited and explained correctly.

In this chapter, we will learn of Paul's understanding of truth, the reasons behind his partial understanding of truth (why he believed what he believed), and we will also discuss and correct interpretations and pinpoint areas of how it is to be applied today.

I want you the reader to know the reason and the basis for the Apostle Paul's limited understanding of revelation regarding this particular area, and they are namely:

1. Personal judgments and convictions

2. Partial understanding of revelation

3. Cultural measurements

In all the different places where Paul was talking about women denied of their privileges to speak and be heard, you would find one or more of these reasons behind them.

CHAPTER SEVEN

Personal Judgments & Convictions

Reading Paul's teaching and some of his strong doctrines that he lays out, it almost seems like we the Church have completely acted out in total rebellion to the word of God by allowing these women preachers to stand behind the pulpit. We have permitted them to finally rise up, to have a say and jeopardize the very plans of God pertaining to the male and female.

I can almost hear some of you thinking that and even quoting the Bible verses to back it up, but wait, suspend your case and read on, and see if the chapters ahead don't answer your sincere questions by the end of each chapter. Please read on because what I am about to reveal in this chapter and the chapters ahead will be an eye opener for you and help you to have a different perspective on reading and understanding the Bible, a healthy one.

Not everything that was handwritten by the Apostle Paul was a direct Revelation of Doctrine from God Almighty.

Not every one of Paul's writings in the Bible should be assumed as direct doctrine from God. They are not! We will find out that some of his writings are based upon his own personal judgments and convictions. He even makes this clear to his readers.

I Corinthians 7:10-Now to the married I command, yet not I but the Lord: A wife is not to depart from her husband.

Regarding issues of marriage relationships, we find Paul making mention of the fact that wives are to stay with their husbands. Notice in that verse Paul makes it clear to the readers that it wasn't some doctrine he created, but that it was the Lord. Now in verse 12, he states the opposite of what he said earlier:

V.S 12- But to the rest I, not the Lord say: if any brother has a wife who does not believe, and she is willing to live with him, let him not divorce her.

He said in verse 10 that it was the Lord but just in verse 12 he said that it was him and not the Lord. This makes it clear that there were times he would be saying, "Thus says the Lord" and other times he would be saying, "Thus says Paul".

The Bible is like a jigsaw puzzle. You have to know how to put the pieces together. The Holy Spirit is just the person for the job. We have to understand that not all the Words given or used are direct words from God. Sometimes they are the writer's own personal judgment of a particular issue he's dealing with. We don't just see the thoughts of God, but also the thoughts of man (man's opinion).

Let us go to our key verse of this subject and make an attempt to shed some light into the subject of Women's freedom, and try to put things back in perspective.

I Timothy 2: 8-14

8: I desire that the men pray everywhere, lifting up Holy hands, without wrath and doubting; 9: in like manner also, that the women adorn themselves in modest apparel, with propriety and moderation, not with braided hair or gold or pearls or costly clothing, 10: but, which is proper for women professing godliness, with good works. 11: Let a woman learn in silence with all submission. 12: And I do not permit a woman to teach or try to have authority over a man, but to be in silence. 13: For Adam was formed first, then Eve. 14: And Adam was not deceived, but the woman being deceived, fell into transgression.

Verse 8 begins with "I will" or "I desire." Could it be that in this verse again, he is supposedly revealing his own personal judgments and convictions and not the direct will of God? I believe so! Not just because of the description of his own will excluding the Lord's Will, but the content of the whole verses of scriptures that come after verse 8; they speak volume of the evidence that it was based on his own judgments and convictions.

Notice the content of the verse, "I will that men pray everywhere, lifting up holy hands, without wrath and doubting." My question is if men don't pray everywhere with hands lifted up, will they be in trouble with the Lord? We all know that we all will be in trouble with that because not too many of us measure up to that standard. Most of the times Christian men are too busy, and some places may not be a suitable place to pray with hands lifted up.

Most work places will not permit that and if it is done so, it can cost them to lose their jobs. We understand that Paul is just making a point and not trying to be literal with his audience. He would want them to get the spirit of it and not in the letter of the law. And by the way, if you haven't been lifting your hands while in prayer; don't get legalistic and feel condemned because you didn't. First, Paul was just making a point, and secondly it was his own judgment or opinion and not the Lord.

Praying everywhere is I think possible. We just have to exercise wisdom or discretion. In the process of seeking to have a presentable environment for prayer and the word, we will need to operate in wisdom and be respective of what house rules the company or your work organization places, so face it, you can't pray there as you would do other places, limitations would be placed on you. Verse 8 should not to be taken literally, however one has to know what manner of spirit Paul is speaking from. What he was saying is men being consistent in prayer and non-compromising.

God is not mad with us for not praying everywhere. It is never a violation of his will, nor is it a quoted scripture from the Bible. You can pray only in your bedroom if that's comfortable for you, you don't have to kneel on your knees if you enjoy prayer walk. I personally don't like kneeling while I'm praying, so I sit on the floor rather. Kneeling hurts my ball and socket joint so I resort to sitting and praying.

According to Paul's personal convictions, that if the men can, then they should lift up Holy hands in prayer to the Lord wherever they are and at all times. He began out by saying; "I want". This tells us that he wanted it. If it's one thing he would want to see in the Church amongst men is that they lift up Holy hands in prayer to God, then how about let's go at it because it's a good thing. However, we need to clearly distinguish between the; "we want", and "when God wants."

We find in this verse of the Scriptures that again it is Paul's own personal judgment and convictions. It is a good thing to get into the habit of praying everywhere with hands lifted up, but in most society and environment it is not going to work. We are not in trouble with God if for some reason we are prevented by the environment to do so. This is what Paul thinks as important for the Body of Christ and it is important. Let me say something to you before we move any further, pray at all times and everywhere if you can!

At the beginning of verse 12 he is again reaffirming to the readers that this was also his own personal convictions and judgments.

I Timothy 2:12 - And I do not permit a Woman to teach or to have authority over a man, but to be in silence.

Notice the words "I do not permit a woman". That part of the verse shows it was the man Paul that disapproves the woman teaching, not God. If it were from God, Paul would have said, "God does not permit a woman". Our first argument is that the reason he said what he said was because of his personal judgment and convictions, and he must've felt that way because of a culture that defined his entire life. It was the way he felt about the women of that day and why? We will discuss more of that as we dive into this book.

I honestly believe that the church of God has no right disapproving and discrediting the woman of our day without a clear analysis of "truth" and "reality". We have to confront every human doctrine, even what we think of as a God doctrine when it could just be cultural or human assumptions. God always has a beneficial reason to what he approves and a non-beneficial reason for the things he disapproves of.

I don't think God would want us to cancel the women gender of our day prematurely without giving much thought to it. The goal of this book is to ask a "why" in every women-limiting barricade and if they don't match up with the whole doctrine of God, especially the complete benefit of the Cross of Jesus, then let us not hold onto, but drop them.

CHAPTER EIGHT

Partial Understanding

Paul really did have mixed feelings and thoughts about the whole issue, having many different reasons that were not concrete. The fact that his own judgments were based not on what God says but on his own convictions is confirmation enough to begin the search for truth and clarity. He received a complete revelation of truth but he must have never experienced the complete renewal of mind from the old underlying knowledge that resided in his subconscious mind.

The old knowledge that he possessed as a Pharisee overrode the new knowledge, which was the revelation that was coming to him. He received as part of the new knowledge Galatians 3: 28, the complete freedom of the female to be regarded as equal with the male. That knowledge did not fully uproot the old knowledge that he had, which was the reason for some of the contradictions in the letters he wrote.

I Timothy 2: 12- is a contradiction: "I do not permit a woman to teach or to have authority over the man".

OLD KNOWLEDGE VERSUS THE NEW

Some of Paul's thoughts reveal the old knowledge he possessed and that he was actually quoting some very interesting points that seem to be the heavy burden on the shoulders of the women of our day. He had a mind "set" toward the traditions and cultures of his day and it was always conflicting with the new understanding that was being revealed to him by the Spirit of God. His mind was yet to be renewed in that area, just like everyone else.

For that (renewing of the mind) to be a reality, time is an important element reconciling the old with the new or perhaps I should say, bringing in the new and out with the old. Does Paul have the luxury of time? No he doesn't, his days like everybody else were numbered to which I believe that had he lived a little longer on this earth, his mind would make sense of the revelation that was coming to him regarding the freedom that God has brought to the Woman of the World. He would then have to be a person who would live at least a good two hundred years, which will be an impossible reality.

Time is a factor when it comes to the revelation of the Word of God. This is like buying a new jacket, after a few weeks you are only able to notice the obvious but as time progresses, with a little extra attention you can begin to see some tags in the inside of the jacket, the marks and details within it. We see more as time progresses. God was patient with humanity all through the years to only give little chunks of revelation one day at a time. Revelation has progressed and advanced more today since the beginning of time and even the beginning of the Church of Jesus Christ our Lord.

Paul's Reasons

WOMEN ARE NOT PERMITED TO TEACH BECAUSE ADAM WAS CREATED FIRST BEFORE EVE

I Timothy 2: 12- And I do not permit a woman to teach or to have authority over a man, but to be in silence.

I Timothy 2: 13- For Adam was formed first, then Eve.

When Paul was writing about his own personal convictions, he gave specific reasons backing his case. The first reason was that Adam was created before Eve was. Here we find the author referring to Genesis as his source and giving the order of authority as part of his reason. In verse 12, he was speaking of the male and female sex. Then, all of a sudden, he switches to the first married couple on planet earth, the very first one since the beginning of time. What we need to understand is that, there is distinction between male and female issue and husband and wife issue. We just cannot mix them all up! In a marriage relationship, the order of authority, the husband being the head of the wife comes into effect. It seem like Paul based from the Jewish culture, was generalizing all female alike, married or not. They are to submit without question to men.

It is not right for anyone to put a single woman in the category of submission along with the married woman. The only place that clearly speaks of woman submitting to a man is if she is married to that man. Outside of the marriage relationship, the woman is not obligated to submit to any man just for the reason that she's a "she", and he's a "he". God did not delegate authority to a man over a woman at the beginning of time because he's a man, but because he's a husband.

Ephesians 5: 22-23 – Wives submit to your husbands, as to the Lord. For the husband is the head of the wife, as also Christ is the head of the Church; and He is the savior of the body.

In Ephesians 5:22 we find that wives are to submit to their husbands, and in verse 23 it says that the husband is the head of the wife. Husbands over wives is what the scripture says, not male over the female. There is not one Scripture in the Bible that supports the theory that a woman ought to submit to the man simply because he's a man. A wife to the husband, yes!

Well, with the exception of a few scriptures that we have been dealing with, from I Timothy and I Corinthians. Here we find Paul's cultural mindset, one that is not totally renewed keeps popping up and spilling over into the boundaries of the revelation that was made available to him for the Body of Christ and in this case, women in particular.

Wherever we find in society that male is accepted to be the head of the female, we have what we call; "Gender Discrimination." When we have that as a governing principle in any setting of life whether it be church, culture, ethnicity, professional or social services, or in any business environment, that would depict: "SEX DISCRIMINATION"!

Authority is only limited in a marriage relationship. When it goes beyond that simply because she's a "she" and he's a "he", and therefore the "he" ought to lead and the "she" submits and listens, then again I say that this is a form of prejudice and gender discrimination. God does not delegate authority to the man over the woman but the husband over the wife. Authority is not a matter of gender but of marriage.

It would be unfair of any reader to generalize all women in the same category with the married women. I think that we have to be clear of why Paul wrote these things to Timothy. The status of the married woman is different from the status of the single woman for the married one is governed by the order of authority.

The authority of the believer speaks to us that the man is the head of the woman and therefore she ought to submit to her husband. Paul in this passage and we will also see from other scripture versus in the New Testament, that his understanding of male and Female gender is filtered by the old knowledge that he attained through the law and culture of his people.

Do not misunderstand me. I am a strong believer in authority and how it is exercised in every area, but I believe that if a man is leading in a certain company and there are women under him, it should be because he's the most qualified and not because he is a male. If a woman is the most qualified, she should be given the same opportunity to apply for chief position of that company. But outside that leadership environment, speaking of marriage life, her husband is the head of her because she is his wife.

Even if she is a wife, it does not mean that she is to be dominated by the husband without question. She can say things to influence and bless the marriage with her pool of knowledge and abilities. The word of God says that she is the "help-meet" for the man, which means that she also has a say in that relationship.

However, Ephesians 5: 25- reveals to us that the wife is to submit to the husband in everything just as the Church does to the Lord Jesus Christ. That portion of scripture seems to sound extreme; it can be used against the women of our day by causing them to suffer without question as they fulfill the scripture by "submitting to everything".

That is not the plan of God for a marriage relationship. Verse 25 is not to be received without verse 26, which says, that the "husbands are to love their wives." Those two scriptures are meant to be embraced together at all times, lived out by both sexes or there's going to be grievances in the relationship, leading to rejection, frustration and, of course, disharmony which will eventually put a strain in the marriage. It takes two to tango! It takes two hands to clap! For if the husband loves the wife he will not abuse that freedom of authority by lording it over her. He will not impose, lay down rules and hammer it down her throat as to make her follow to the letter the finest detail as we have witnessed in most cultures, but he will rather assist and work together, and complement each other.

My wife **loves to submit** more than she thinks it's a **duty to submit.** How and why is that? When a woman is loved by actions, she is moved to respect the wishes, intents and leadings of the head (husband). She notices the love and out of appreciation she gives and gives, and the husband reciprocates. Husbands and wives complete and complement each other rather than competing against each other. Husband and wife relationship is not about power struggle. It's about love and harmony, which leads to the genuine observance of the order of Authority. The genuine observance of the order of authority stems out of the attitude that says; "I want to" not "I have to."

It is the same way in the church. If the wife has a calling of God on her life to pastor a church, the husband is to respect his wife as the head of the church, but at home it is the husband who is the head and the wife will have to give the husband what is due to him. In this case, the woman is anointed to be the pastor of the Church, but the husband, the head of the wife.

Let me add by saying that I do not believe that a wife can be anointed to be the head of the husband. She's probably anointed with butter if she is, not with the anointing of the Spirit of God. This is a violation of the order of authority and God is not behind it 100%, as for this lifestyle is also running wild today like a mad man. The freedom of women has its extremes as well.

There are women today who do not want to get married because they do not want to be under a man's authority. I say fine! This is still a better way to live than to be married and run your husband out of office. That would be a coup-de-tat! A coup conducted by the spirit of Jezebel! What is the spirit of Jezebel? This is the spirit that controls and manipulates leadership.

It is the spirit that destroys families, churches, organizations and any group setting that requires leadership. The spirit of Jezebel doesn't necessarily require woman to do his bidding for this spirit uses man, assistants, secretaries, boards, deacons and the list goes on and on. The spirit of Jezebel will always seek to breed in an environment where it can control or manipulate leadership.

Paul's first reason is not a weighty enough reason to build a case against the women of our day. It may be a rule of conduct for some society back then in the day of the Bible, but it is definitely not for today. Let me assure you that once we begin to unfold the revelation of the Works of the Cross of Jesus, we will then understand why these things are written by the Apostle Paul and how important it is not to get caught up with the mechanical legalistic side of it. Let's go to the next reason:

WOMEN ARE NOT PERMITED TO SPEAK BECAUSE THEY ARE THE DECEIVED

The second reason Paul gave and like the first one, he also brought his information from the same source supporting his first reason, Genesis chapters 1-2 & 3:

I Timothy 2:14- And Adam was not deceived, but the woman being deceived was in transgression.

What is he talking about here? Paul is talking about another reason why a woman should not teach a man and that is because she was the one deceived and not the man. I also believe that Paul categorizes all women as the very cause of sin and that they are in no position to try and teach since they are the unqualified ones.

Notice, he was drawing women's weakness from the first ever sin in the World that had involved Eve, a woman. He is saying that after Adam and Eve's sin, every woman now has a tendency to mess up and to do the same. Another interesting point to note is that Women are spoken of in here, not the married ones, but women in general. This is to confirm what I introduced in the last chapter, regarding Paul's viewpoint towards women, and how they are generalized in the same category, whether married or not.

After giving his first reason of Adam being the first created, then Eve, he then brought the second reason as to why woman was not to teach nor make an attempt to usurp authority over the man. His second reason was that the woman was the one deceived and not the man. If I may paraphrase: " a woman ought not to teach a man because she is the weaker one, more messed up than the man, and has a greater tendency to sin because Eve was a woman and so every woman is the same."

Let's look up the source from *Genesis 3:17*

And unto Adam he said, Because thou has hearkened unto the voice of thy wife, and has eaten of the tree, of which I commanded saying, Thou shall not eat of it: cursed is the ground for thy sake; in sorrow shall thou eat of it all the days of thy life;

When we read that portion of the scripture, it almost sound like God was saying to Adam after they committed high treason that he (Adam) was not supposed to listen to the woman at all. It is as if she was handed a final decree on that particular day that because she was the one tempted, she should not be allowed to ever open her mouth to try and teach or usurp authority over the man.

That is not true. God was not making a decree in that portion of the scripture. What He was actually saying was that in that moment of time, Adam's mistake was that after having known the truth, he didn't say "No" to Eve's invitation but welcomed them wholeheartedly, permitting the woman to overrule his decision. Adam knew that it was a sin and a violation, but he listened to his wife anyway.

He knew it was wrong but he went along with it. It wasn't an eternal decree to all the women of our day as what it may sound like, pertaining to what Paul mentioned in his letters to Timothy. What happened in the Garden of Eden wasn't reason enough to generalize all women the same. That may be true for the Jewish people in accordance with their culture, but it is definitely not for you, being a gentile, and speaking of the death, burial, resurrection and ascension of Jesus, I can boldly say it's not even for the Jews.

As you may have picked up by now, that I keep pointing to the death, burial and resurrection of Jesus in Chapters ahead because we will then see how things have truly changed because of the fulfillment of His mission (Redemption). Jesus Christ came and has made a difference, we just don't know it yet. The Word does not say that the truth will set us free. It's to know the truth that brings freedom.

It was Adam's terrible mistake for listening and deciding to do wrong at that moment of time when he already very well knew to do the right thing but didn't. So what God said was that Adam could have stopped the damage had he not listen to Eve talking him into sin. What He was not saying though, was that women in all generations are not supposed to speak at all because of being the first to sin. We must not use such scriptures as a foundation scripture of blaming the woman and generalizing them all as one. Like the first reason the second is invalid and irrelevant because firstly, it is not right, and secondly which is the most important reason: what Jesus came and do, by dying on the Cross a little over two thousand years ago.

Paul was not only speaking to the different cultures that interrelate and they were the Jewish, Roman and Ephesians cultures. But he was also influenced by these cultures. He not only spoke to those three cultures but to all the cultures of the World, and to all the women of the World. He was looking at all the women with a cultural grid mindset.

He measured the woman's issue culturally. Could it be that Paul's culture grid where he filters the issue regarding women is plainly invalid? Could it be that the reasons, which Paul gave were just his own judgment and personal convictions for which no one must adhere to? I believe so! It would also be wrong of you, the female reader, to think that these strong words of Paul are yours to identify with. Keep reading because we are building our foundation for what's coming in the later chapters, what's coming is the difference that Christ brought for the people of the World, women included.

Summing up my conclusions you will understand the complete picture of what the will of God is for you. What the Will of God is for you, the Christian woman and any woman reading this book is to be free to do what God has laid in your heart. I know it almost seems like I'm disregarding Paul's work. In actual fact, I'm just bringing clarity to God's will through the awesome work of Paul the Apostle, and to make sure that countless women all around the World are not hung up by those few scriptures. It was Paul's work that brought the Church to where it is today. His work is so detailed about the works of the Cross of Jesus, and the benefits that follow.

CHAPTER NINE

Cultural Measurements

When we started discussing cultural measurements at the beginning of the book, we had not really talked about it in detail even though it was very much present in every chapter. It is also found in almost every book of the Bible. Paul's letter to Timothy reveals a Jewish culture dominating Paul's theology and when he mentions the two reasons based from Genesis, we need to understand that they were culturally inspired. The Jewish society, yes and even the Gentile World, is what the author expected to communicate in this message.

So what are cultural measurements? Cultural measurements occur when the author begins to make his argument based on his culture and custom, measuring his understanding of the subject with the culture of his time. We have to understand the author of these startling books (epistles) is so well informed in the things about his culture, religion and social climate of that day.

The Children of Israel were given strict rules by God to preserve this way of life that He gave them, to preserve and pass down from one generation to another and never to lose it for anything in the world.

God was so serious about these matters that He commanded them to write this new way of life, instructions on the wall, on the door of their houses, posts and even on their hands as a reminder.

Deuteronomy 6: 6- 9

And these words, which I command you today, shall be in your heart. You shall teach them diligently to your children, and shall talk of them when you sit in your house, when you walk by the way, when you lie down, and when you rise up. You shall bind them as a sign on your hand, and they shall be as frontlets between your eyes. You shall write on the doorposts of your house and on your gates.

The Children of Israel were forbidden to intermarry with other nations. They were only to marry other Israelites, someone of their own kind, as a way of preserving their newfound way of life.

The years, months, days, and seasons became special because they had everything to do with their new way of life. Everything about the Israelites' way of life was modified: the hairdos, the dress code, and even their behavior. This way of life became an integral part of their whole life; a custom, then a tradition passed down from generations and generations to come. It becomes so unnatural not to live up to these traditions. What is natural and normal is to live and preserve the culture of the day.

When addressing the issues about women, Paul had some strong cultural mindset of the Jewish culture although he applied some of the revelation knowledge given him to change some life absorbing culture of his own people. He subconsciously held to this culture pertaining to woman and was combining some of the new knowledge with them. This was evident in some of his writings about woman for in some places he would agree with equality, and in others he would disagree. It seems like he was giving out a mixed message.

Just look up this interesting verse:

I Corinthians 11: 13-14-15-16

13 Judge among your selves. Is it proper for a woman to pray to God with her head uncovered? 14 Does not even nature itself teach that if man has long hair, it is a dishonor to him? 15 But if a woman has long hair, it is a Glory to her; for her hair is given to her for a covering. 16- But if anyone seems to be contentious, we have no such custom, nor do the Churches of God.

This passage speaks about the Jewish tradition regarding how the women and men's physical appearance is modified to carry symbolic meaning of the relationship between God and men, and men and women. There are more details about the passage that I will not elaborate on, but I want to bring your attention to a specific Scripture.

Verse 14 says that for a man to have long hair is not natural and it is a disgrace to them.

This is a disgrace to the Jewish culture.

It is unnatural not to be living according to the Jewish culture. It is not normal by the standards of man; it is unacceptable and a complete disgrace. The point is that Paul measured some of his findings culturally, by the standard the Jewish culture was observed and preserved. In verse 13, he was urging his readers to judge among themselves whether this is acceptable by the standards of man or not.

Paul's judgment about women was both measured and inspired by his culture (the culture of the day). Some have written that what Paul said was only directed to the Jews and not the Gentile World. Even if that is true, that it is directed only to the Jews, aren't they human beings and aren't they deeply in need of freedom too just like everybody else? Yes, and so it happened Christ died for them also. Christ died for the whole World.

Statistics given by ABC news in 2008 states that 80% of the middle-eastern women suffer from domestic violence. For these middle-eastern women, the majority of those suffering are from the Islam faith. Most of the women are suffering silently because they believe Allah intends for them to submit without question. Their basic rights are stripped away from them, and for them to speak out would mean being violently abused or even death.

Women is a commodity. They are just like a piece of furniture.

The greater Islam Women feels that way regarding how they are treated by their male.

Mussarat Misbah

Freedom is the most sought after quality in the whole world. You wonder why so many people flock to the United States of America. They are tired of tyranny, unjust treatment, abuse, and of course, sexual discrimination. People are born to be free and America is one of the countries that have sheltered so many wounded and are fleeing the oppression of the countries they have left.

The one good thing about America is that you can be all you want to be and nobody will stand in the way, by ways of deprivation, depriving you of being the person you always wanted to be. There is however a flip side to that coin. Freedom can also become a license for sin. Regardless of how we may respond to freedom God still wants for humans to be free, for them to come willingly to him and not with a strong hand. We in our freedom can choose to desire purity or we can choose to indulge in the carnal appetites of the flesh. God's given us the freedom to choose him or not to, and He will not make anyone serve Him! Most Americans, don't realize how fortunate they are to be born in America.

Some have complained about America, pointed a finger at America and yes there are things that America would stand guilty of. But isn't the Whole World a place of imperfections, nations and people alike? No, not one nation of the world is excluded from defects. Most Americans do not have a healthy respect for America because they have never lived in a third world country where individual human rights are suppressed or ignored.

They are, sometimes, not necessarily third World countries but countries where dictatorial type leadership rule, a country where democracy is thrown out the window. Too many of the people living in these countries are living a life of constant battle for survival every day, whether it's fighting terrorism, communism, sex discrimination, starvation or whatever there is to fight off. Humans can only put up with so much, and then they flee it or retaliate.

Black civil activist James Farmer JR, one of the "big four" leaders of the American Civil Rights Movement quoted St Augustine in one of his early speeches and added a few quotations to that of St Augustine's: "An Unjust law is no law at all" which means I have a right, even a duty to resist. With violence or civil disobedience! You should pray I choose the latter

Retaliation through violence to an unjust system, civil disobedience or fleeing it is sign of a quest for freedom in the human heart. Refugees that flee to America feel a relief that one can almost say; "it feels like coming to Heaven." Not just America, but other developed countries such as Canada, Australia, New Zealand and many more which have accepted refugees. God bless these countries of the World! Every human being seeks after freedom and freedom is every human beings entitlement. Let freedom reign!

CHAPTER TEN

As The Law Says

I Corinthians 14:34-Let your woman keep silent in the Churches, for they are not permitted to speak; but they are to be submissive, as the Law also says. 35 and if they want to learn something let them ask their own husbands at home; for it is "shameful for women to speak in Church".

In his letter to the Corinthian Church, Paul brought the subject up again, probably because of the disorder in worship and the operation of the gifts in the Churches. He spoke of examples, how more than one person was giving prophetic utterances at the same time instead of waiting for a turn, and not interrupting the other person who is flowing in the gifts.

The spirit of a prophet subjects himself to the prophet. Everything has to be conducted in a spirit of love, unity, and order for God is a God of order. While reminding the church about order in terms of worship in the church, Paul immediately switches to the same topic of the woman of that day and begins to set the record straight, saying that **they are not permitted to speak in Churches (Verse 34).**

Why would Paul bring up the subject about the women in the middle of his writing about the gifts and how they are to be utilized and used within the boundaries of order in worship? This is simple. For women to try lifting their voice in the utilization of their gifts, whether it is prophecy, leading, preaching or teaching, it is totally unacceptable, and is regarded as creating not just a disorder in worship but a violation of the law.

They are completely forbidden from participating in these types of worship services, in terms of attempting to speak or teach. The Law as the scripture says forbids them, which is the very reason why the rules that were laid down by Paul regarding the women. He was not only basing his judgments from the fact that he was speaking to the other two cultures (Ephesus & Rome), but mostly the Jewish laws.

<u>On the grounds of interpretation, immediate contextual scriptures take priority over historical and cultural background.</u>

What has happened before (**history**) may not be what's happening now (**context**). History is always a great basis for the interpretation of the scriptures, but it's not the only way; there are other grounds for interpreting the scripture. History should not override the immediate context of the scripture. Some believe that they were forbidden to speak because they were sitting from a different section and were trying to ask questions to which they were then silenced, basing judgment on what may have happened (History). This is pure speculation!

Immediate context is verse 34b of I Corinthians 14: "**for they are not permitted to speak**" and verse 35b: "**for it is shameful for them to speak at Church.**"

The assumption of authors and theologians is something that may have really happened and it may have happened in the past, but not according to what I see (immediate context) in the scriptures. Again the assumption was based on the women making too much noise, which is a disharmony in the order of the service, but it wasn't disorderly in the service that they were accused of; it was a violation of the law.

I Corinthians 14: 34b- for they are not permitted to speak, but to be submissive, as the law says.

It wasn't a disharmony in the order of service that Paul was addressing; it was a violation of the law!

The law forbids them to speak! To exegete the scriptures, one must not look only to what is historical and miss the contextual, or in this case, to miss the immediate context and related versus due to focus on the distant context of the entire chapter. I think that most Christian authors are missing it because they focus on the distant context rather than on the immediate and nearest context.

Forbidden by law is the motivation for which Paul brought this correction to the women. This here is the immediate context as was in verses 34 & 35. They were not silenced because they were making too much noise but because they were considered unfit for this Holy task. A task discharged by men only. It's like the acronym, "GOLF", Gentlemen Only Ladies Forbidden. The acronym "GOLF" is just a joke gone wild. That is not the true meaning of the word "golf" and the origin of this old Scottish sport is unknown. I'm just making a point that ladies were forbidden under the Old T just like the acronym GOLF. John Stott in his book the story of the New Testament elaborates on the women in the land of Israel as unfit candidates in studying the Bible correctly.

Again, the one Question that bears repetition: "Why were they forbidden from speaking?" Verse 34 gives us the reason. It is a part of fulfilling the law that was their custom, culture and of course, tradition. What do we find here? We find the author again basing his judgments from cultural measurements, the governing law of the Jewish society. It is the ordinances or rule of law serving as a culture, religious tradition that was passed down through all their people, from one generation to the next.

In verse 35 he was saying the same thing again: **"it is a shame",** which literally gives us the idea that to violate such rule is to breach the social, political, cultural, and religious standard of the day. The law that was handed to them by God caused the external modification of their whole life. They preserved it then as a culture and a custom that was observed and passed down as a tradition.

As we begin to understand the connections and be provided with a broader description of the will of God and the works of the Cross of Christ, I can confidently say that true freedom without another ounce of weight on our shoulder will be ours to own! Praise God forever more! According to the law; Leviticus 12:1-8 speaks of the different cleansing periods and stages both male and female must go through.

Leviticus 12: 1- 8

Then the Lord spoke to Moses saying, " speak to the children of Israel, saying; 'If a woman has conceived, and borne a child, then she shall be unclean seven days; as in the days of her customary impurity she shall be unclean. And on the eighth day the flesh of his foreskin shall be circumcised. She shall then continue in the blood of her purification thirty-three days. She shall not touch any hallowed thing, nor come into the sanctuary until the days of her purification are fulfilled. But if she bears a female child, then she shall be unclean two weeks, as in her customary impurity, and she shall continue in the blood of her purification sixty-six days. When the days of her purification are fulfilled, whether for a son or a daughter, she shall bring to the priest a lamb of the first year as a burnt offering, and a young pigeon or a turtle dove as a sin offering, to the door of tabernacle of meeting. Then he shall offer it before the Lord, and make atonement for her. And she shall become clean from the flow of her blood. This is the law for her who has borne a male or female. And if she is not able to bring a lamb, then she may bring two turtledoves or two young pigeons - one as a burnt offering and the other as a sin offering. So the priest shall make atonement for her, and she will be clean.

There are a lot of details in this whole chapter that I do not want to get into, some information that is not relevant to this topic at all. But I want to draw your attention to a couple of verses.

In verses 1 through 4, we find the cleansing time periods of mothers who have given birth to a baby child, whether male or female. If the child is a male, first the mother would be considered unclean for a week and then the overall cleansing time period for her would be 33 days. If the child is a female, the mother would be considered unclean for two weeks and her total cleansing period would be 66 days.

With the male child, the mother has to undergo cleansing only for herself, but with the female child, the mother undergoes cleansing both for her sake and for her daughter. The period of time of cleansing is automatically doubled which tells us that the male is considered pure and clean all the way from birth to adulthood provided he keeps himself pure, whereas the female is considered unclean all the way from birth to adulthood. The female is despised and regarded as unclean among the Jewish people, a total outcast, and the farthest away from God Almighty.

As according to the story of the New Testament: By John Stott

Luke and his message: Pg 49 Concern for people on the margins

2 a: Women. Women had little social status in the Roman Empire, and in contemporary Jewish, they were equally degraded.

One of the daily rabbinic thanksgivings was: **"Blessed art thou, O Lord God, Who hast not made me a slave, a gentile or a woman."** Scribes and Pharisees would avoid talking to women in public, and many of them held that women were incapable of studying the Scriptures correctly.

It's no wonder why they are told to ask of their husbands at home rather than inquiring in Church.

Notice that they were totally degraded by both the Jewish culture and the Roman Empire. (The Roman Empire was the governing authority of the day).

Scribes and Pharisees would avoid talking to women in public.

They were also incapable of studying the Scriptures correctly.

The scribes and Pharisees avoid talking to women in public because of a Jewish cultural tradition that they observe. It is a law of conduct. Both the Scribes and Pharisees are a hierarchy class of the Jewish people. They seem to possess a greater knowledge of the Laws of God.

Seeing them avoiding talking to the Women indicate that they conduct themselves in such a manner superior than the average Jew especially the women, because of the knowledge of the law that they posses and function from. They behave in a certain way because of what they know and believe. Knowledge is the unseen force behind the actions which acts as manifestation of the unseen.

Jesus own words were; "You shall judge them by its fruit", you don't have fruit at the top of a tree unless there is seed in the ground. **If Fruits mean action, then the law would be seeds.** The law as Paul mentioned was the code of conduct amongst the Jewish society. The laws that God Almighty gave them were written on properties and even on themselves, what they do say is influenced and shaped by the Laws of God. Their whole life is modified to read what the Law says. Their whole life exemplifies the laws of God.

They were incapable of studying the Scriptures correctly.

Is this the reason why Paul forbade the women from speaking in the Churches, why he mentioned that they are not to try and teach, why he mentioned that it is shameful amongst women to do so? Definitely! Paul based on his Jewish cultural mindset, projected that they are the weaker ones because Eve, a woman, was created second, they are easily tempted because Eve was deceived and not Adam. Moreover, they are incapable of studying scriptures correctly.

An important thought to note; if one is incapable of studying correctly why should he or she try and teach because it will only lead to error and most likely heresy. That is how the women were perceived back then amongst the Jewish society. They are close to err, and incapable of embracing the truth for they were the tempted and not the men. This is the culture that Paul was speaking of and I happen to believe that he was addressing these matters in his letters. Notice these summaries again:

What we've learnt about the Jewish Women so far.

 a) Women must be silent

 b) They must not teach their men or the Church of God

 c) If they do have a question, they are to ask their husbands at home.

 d) They were more unclean than the male

 e) They were incapable of studying the scriptures correctly

 f) They were classified along with the Slaves and the Gentiles.

 g) Have very little social status and as equally degraded as the Roman women are.

 h) Priests and Pharisees avoid talking to them in public.

Those eight things reveal clearly the treatment of women during the days of the early church and during the rule of the Roman Empire. It was a pop culture of the day.

The statement that sums it all up is the prayer of the Rabbi's, **"Blessed art thou O Lord God, who hast not made me a slave, a gentile or a women."**

Notice how the women are categorized and classified along with slaves and gentiles, the known to be unclean. That is a woman under the Old Covenant. It can also be the identity of the women under the New Covenant if for any reason in the world, not having to understand the complete revelation of the works of the Cross.

The apostle Paul wrote with great deal of convictions, but in his letters where he mentioned women's restraining order, he wrote things that is still tied up to the culture of his day, and even backs them with scripture. And why is this? It was literally an overflow of partial understanding. He had some partial understanding of the known will of God.

Not that he was wrong or that his teaching needs to be removed from the Bible, but realizing that most of what he said about women is so unacceptable to this day and age, because of the culture he was speaking from and to the two time periods considered plus the level of understanding knowledge of that day.

Cultures, as we know them, have evolved. Back in the day when I was a little boy, tattoos was only worn by criminals but today lawyers, doctors, police officers and many other professions put them on their bodies.

To some culture tattoo is a taboo, but for the Samoans those of the chiefly family wear it. Fiji is a very religious country, a country I called home until at least 9 years ago for when I relocated to a different country. The first three years to the new country was very difficult for me because of culture shock. I saw some Christian brothers wearing tattoos and I was disturbed although the designs were clean and Christian. My religious background coupled with pop culture taught me that this was wrong but I felt very helpless, judgmental and confused.

Where was God in all of these, what was His reactions? Is he not judging these people? This is an abomination!

After a time of contemplating further on the subject, I realized that God wasn't interested in the technicality of the diverse culture by holding this against their worship and love for Him. God says; "come as you are." I personally do not think that God is freaking out at the changes hitting the 21st century. God is a God of ethnicity and culture. Culture is just evolving. A wonderful prophetic verse that reveals the God that sees the end from the beginning, even compliments the ever-evolving pop culture.

Isaiah 44:4- 6 Amplified Bible

And they shall spring up among grass like the willows or poplars by the watercourses. One will say, I am the Lord's; and another will call himself by the name of Jacob; and another will write [even brand or tattoo] upon his hand, I am the Lord's, and surname himself by the (honorable) name of Israel. Thus says the Lord, King of Israel and his redeemer, the Lord of hosts: I am the first and I am the last; besides me there is no God.

Here three groups are mentioned. The first group is the traditional Christians because they call themselves by the name of the Lord and are different from the third group. The second would definitely be the Jews and the Messianic Jews because they call themselves by the name of Jacob who is an Israelite, and the last ones are some from the 21st century Christians who have embraced the change of popular culture, because the name of the Lord is written (tattooed) on their hands.

In verse 7, God mentions and describe Him as the first and the last, which literally means that He has not only seen the past and the present saints but also the future saints. We are freaking out by what we see in this new breed of saints that is storming the shores of Christianity with an unorthodox wave of change! God Himself isn't freaking out at this new thing, in fact he compliments and categorizes them alongside the more orthodox ones. He mentions in verse 8 that they all are His witnesses.

CHAPTER ELEVEN

God's blowing Winds of Change!

Whether we like it or not, God is bringing in the winds of change so we, as the 21st century saints can tackle the task of bringing a people group that's well versed with pop-culture to the Cross of Jesus Christ. The Church popular culture is not at the crossroads of change; it is already in the middle of it! Church pop-culture is evolving, and I believe that it is so for the sake of having our voice heard. God uses all mediums for the sake of the preaching of the Gospel of Jesus.

We are called to be a down-to-earth people, not low downs, strange not weird, separated from worldly influences but not isolated! Pertaining to women, the culture surrounding them has changed and yes, some of them are pastors of Churches and the husbands are filling roles of co-pastors rather. Today they become CEO's, senators, board members and even vice-presidents.

The year 2009, the first lady to former president Clinton, Hillary Clinton almost became the first women President in the United States of America. Let's face it, the women are not what they used to be, they have evolved and are coming out of their closet. God almighty is not reacting to such a change, He responds to it with intelligence and love. In fact, He is behind the change in spite of all the extremes that have come out of it.

God was patient with mankind, not forcing His way into the lives of mankind understanding that revelation is progressive. What Paul knew then about women was beneficial for the Body of Christ to build on understanding correct knowledge, so the Church of all times can enjoy the liberty of the Spirit through women. All I'm using is directly from the woodwork, all from Paul's life work.

They played major clues to my understanding of the woman's complete freedom.

THE UNCLEAN

I want to get you to focus your attention on this diagram for a moment. That is the, "Holy of Holies."

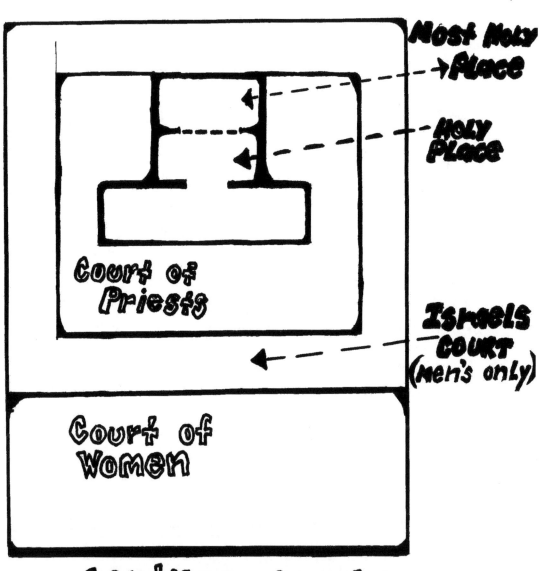

drawing by Author of Book

In the diagram above, there are five specific rooms that reveal people's classification and their position before a Holy God. The Holiest of all is the place where God is and only one individual gets to enter into it once a year. That one individual is the High Priest who is an (anti type) representing the role Jesus would come and play when He died and entered the Holiest of all once and for all. He was the only one who went into the Holy of Holies (The real sanctuary in Heaven) to offer up His sacrificial blood once and for all.

The next room is the Holy place where all the other priests are restricted to, and faithfully perform their priesthood services. The third room would be Israel's court, men's only. The fourth one is known to be the women's court, and then lastly is the outer court or the Gentile's court. The closest individual to the Holy of Holies is the purest of all according to the law who is the High Priest, and even in his purity he still offers up sacrifice both for himself and his people once every year. He is the anti-type of Jesus Christ Himself. He only represents the only one individual qualified for the Holiest of all whose blood is the purest of all blood sacrifice.

He (Jesus) entered into the Holiest of all only once and no other sacrifice is necessary because it is the only perfect sacrifice that has paid in full all debt. Notice in the diagram that the women are not together with the men, but that they are the closest to the Gentiles. It is no wonder they are regarded as the unclean, the not qualified and amongst the Israelites, they are the farthest from God's presence.

All this is just confirming every detail we've talked about concerning the condition of women under the old covenant, under the law and in the culture of that day. Wow! It makes complete sense why a woman should not be behind the pulpit at all. Yeah but wait; we've already established that under the New Testament this was not a direct word from God but a personal conviction of one man based upon his understanding of the law, his culture and traditions and probably was directed only to the Jewish people.

Furthermore, what I am about to bring to your understanding will and should change your whole thinking about women, how that Christ has come in and made a difference, setting people free from all walks of life regardless of what bondage of slavery they might be tied up to. Get ready to be renewed in your thinking and be transformed into the image of God's Son Jesus Christ. Prepare yourselves to receive the ultimate truth, the truth that dispels all doubt and removes the bondage and burden of legalism. The truth that introduces individual Christian women to a life of confidence and determination to be all they could be in Christ Jesus.

CHAPTER TWELVE

Jesus Makes The Difference!

Keeping the diagram in focus, Jesus died outside of the Tabernacle's gate, Calvary cross stood on what the Bible describes as the Gentile's territory. The outside of the camp is the place for the unclean, the dogs or the uncircumcised.

Hebrews-13: 10- 13

We have an altar from which those who serve the tabernacle have no right to eat. For the bodies of those animals, whose blood is brought into the sanctuary by the High Priest for sin, are burned outside the camp. Therefore Jesus also, that He might sanctify the people with His own blood, suffered outside the gate. Therefore let us go forth to Him, outside the camp, bearing His reproach.

Versus 10 & 11 states that Jesus died outside of the city, the place of the Gentile's territory which is the place of the outcast, the worst of all human beings, the most unclean and the ones who are the farthest from God. Why? Why didn't he die in the area of just the Israel's court? Well if that was to be the case, then both the women's and the Gentiles would be left out of the blessings of the Cross of Jesus Christ. If that were to be the case, then there would not be any salvation for the women and the Gentiles.

He died in the court of the Gentiles and then carried his own sacrificial blood all the way from there to the Holiest of all, which then makes every other court with its people along the way all cleansed and accepted before God the Father. Jesus was not going to leave even the least one out or behind. Praise God Almighty! He started from the outside in, from down up. He started with the Gentile world breaking down all barriers of separation, all the way to the Holy of Holies and presented his blood as evidence that all debt is paid in full. There is hope for the lowest sinner, and everyone in between

In Hebrews 9:12, the author speaks to us of how Jesus after his resurrection entered into the most Holy place to obtain eternal redemption through his own blood. Mathew 27:50-51- gives us an event that took place during Jesus' death on the cross, which is directly symbolic to what is happening at that very moment of time.

Mathew 27:50-51-And Jesus cried out again with a loud voice, and yielded up his Spirit. Then, behold, the veil of the temple was torn in two from top to bottom; and the earth quaked, and the rocks split,

What happened was directly symbolic, revealing that all veils of separation, all veils that seem to discriminate the other party, and all veils that determine which ones are closer to God and which ones are not has all been pulled down and taken away forever. Glory to God in the highest!

Reverend Kenneth E Hagin quoted these words regarding the event:

"The scriptural accounts don't say that the temple was rent in twain or torn in two from bottom to top. They say it was rent from top to bottom. Some unseen being - an angel of God twenty feet up in the air ripped it apart downward. And God would never again dwell within a man made Holy of Holies. He would dwell in the believers, the Body of Christ."

The Spirit Within and The Spirit Upon. Chapter 11 Pg 152

"When the veil was torn, it meant two things: the Spirit has now left His throne and have access to living in us, also we can now have access into God's Holy presence."

Taken from one of Kenneth Hagin's Victory magazine:

Year magazine was published is unknown.

Not only that, but by the revelation of the Spirit to Paul, we also have access to one another. All barriers that separates one from another has all been pulled down, the ones that remain standing are men-formulated barriers or the ones standing due to a lack of understanding revelation knowledge. Hosea 4: 6 gives us this; "my people are destroyed because of lack of knowledge."

The Spirit not only has access to us. We also have access to God and access to one another. Everybody has become equal in the sight of God, regardless of race, gender or color, Christ has become all in all.

Ephesians 2: 11-12-13-14-15-16-17- 18 (NIV Bible translation)

Therefore remember that you, once were Gentile in the flesh- who are called un-circumcision by what is called the circumcision made in the flesh by hands that at that time you were without Christ, being Aliens from the commonwealth of Israel and foreigners to the Covenant of promise, having no hope and without God in this world. But now in Christ Jesus you who once were far off have been brought near by the blood of Christ. For He Himself is our peace, who has made both one, and has broken down the middle wall of separation, having abolished in His flesh the enmity, that is the law of commandments contained in ordinances, so as to create in Himself one new man from the two, thus making peace, and that He might reconcile them both to God in one body through the Cross, thereby putting to death the enmity. And He came and preached peace to you who are far off and to those who were near. For through Him we both have access by one Spirit to the Father.

In these verses, we find the writer of Ephesians making mention of the fact that there is definitely a barrier of separation between Jews and Gentiles. In verse 12, he begins to speak a little about having to become one with the Jews even in our Gentile state, which can only be possible through Christ's death alone. Now notice in verse 14, the barriers of separation in the temple was taken away and that everyone can have access to God by himself or herself without the help of the priests.

He or She has become the priest of one's own self as was confirmed by Peter in His letter (I Peter 2: 9), "a royal priesthood." We are all Priests and therefore need not confess our sins to a Priest/ a Father, but to God almighty Himself! Hallelujah! I can come before God Himself and commune with Him concerning every little detail about my life!

Also the tearing down of the veil permits us to have access to one another without discriminating the other party, the standing barrier has been taken away. He has made the two as one. Hebrews 9:24 tells us that the temple or the Holy of Holies is just a copy of the real thing, so everything within the boundary of the temple seem to have a significant meaning. The **barriers that separate**, the very ones that were torn down through the death, burial and resurrection of Jesus represent the **legalistic laws of commandments contained in ordinances.**

The Jewish legalistic system brought separation, the woman in particular were considered the unclean for which they have to live separately from the man, and the barriers reveal their being pushed away as an outcast. They have no part in the Presence of God. The Legalistic laws, that bound women says; "you cannot because you are", and thus keeps them away from the liberty of the Sons of God.

As Paul furthered his writings in Ephesians 2 after making mention of the pulling down of the barriers of separation in verse 14, then begins to explain the meaning of the barriers in the following verse 15.

Ephesians 2: 15- By His death He ended the angry resentment between us, caused by the Jewish laws which favored the Jews and excluded the Gentiles, for He died to annul the whole system of Jewish laws. Then He took the two groups that were opposed to each other and made them parts of Himself; thus He fused us together to become one new person, and at last there was peace. (New Living Bible Translation)

In that verse alone, a whole lot of information is beginning to make sense, the Jewish system that was an angry resentment between the two parties Jews and Gentiles, only favored the Jews. The same system categorizes and classifies even the Jewish women along with the Gentiles.

Notice the latter part of that verse, "dying to annul the whole Jewish system and then making all the different parties become one by becoming Himself." Having the temple in mind, all barriers have been torn down which means the taking away of the whole Jewish system. All have learnt to come together through the one common ground, "Jesus", despite the differences each party possesses.

Not Just One Veil But all.

Ephesians 2: 17 -And He came and preached peace to you who were afar off and to those who were near.

In light of the temple, the farthest are the Gentiles and the closest are the priests. So if He (Jesus) preaches to the farthest and the closest, **then everyone in between is also included in the peace message. Who all are the parties in between as according to their classifications? They are the Jewish men and women. With each group there is a standing veil that separates and all of these veils have been torn down for which they have peace with one another and with God. Men and Women can sit together and both can worship God any way they like, Gentiles can sit with them and worship God freely. What God has cleansed by His blood and approves let no man disqualify.**

But what has the message preached? What is the peace message?

The message is found in verse -13. But now in Christ you who were once far away have been brought near by the Blood of Christ.

God has called the farthest to come close to him, which in particular are the Gentiles and the Jewish women. The barriers are taken away, and everyone is categorized no longer by their race or gender; they are all categorized by being one in Christ Jesus.

The message is plain and simple, everyone is equal in the sight of God because everyone is accepted and justified in the sight of God.

Clean as the Lord Jesus is.

All can walk right into the Holy of Holies without guilt or condemnation. Because God has accepted the Gentiles, He has even accepted the Jewish women as clean as Jesus is. That's the cleanest one can ever get, as clean as Jesus is and we all are as clean as Jesus. Everyone that has accepted Jesus has become as clean and righteous as Jesus. It is interesting to note that the Gentiles are not made to be as clean as the Jews or the women as clean as the men, or even the little priests. But they were all made to be as clean as Jesus!

They are made to be clean in the level of cleanliness God Himself inhabits. If you are accepted by God then don't let no one judge you what you should and should not do. Women, you too can do what men do, you too can preach, pastor a Church or head a company. As a matter of fact God has called some of you into these leadership positions. God does not judge you for doing so. Free at last! Free at last! Shout once you know that you are free at last! Be all that your heart craves to do, that significant somebody that God has created you to be.

After that great and marvelous doing of God Almighty by pulling down all standing barriers in the temple, and bringing together all the parties that once lived in total discrimination through the corruptive Jewish system of laws and regulations, Galatians 3:28 becomes a reality:

"There is neither Jew nor Greek, slave nor free, male nor female, for you are all one in Christ Jesus."

Earlier in our book we discussed how that part of the Rabbi's Prayer really speaks of discriminating the three groups, and they are the Gentiles or Greeks, the Slaves and the Women. Well the Good News is that these three groups, according to Galatians 3:28 have been accepted and have become one with the accepted.

This present teaching alone nullify the theory that women should not preach in the Churches. Paul's teaching to Timothy about women is invalid for today's application where they are not permitted to speak in the Churches. I believe they are quite beneficial at his time due to the amount of revelation knowledge they possess, considering the culture of their time then, but it is definitely not for our day.

There are some people who say; "Paul is only addressing the Jews", I say it's not even for the Jews to observe because Jesus died to take away the laws that brought discrimination not only to the Jews, but also to all the different societies classified by the Law which includes Jewish women.

CHAPTER THIRTEEN
The Qualifying Component

The priests along with Kings and Prophets were the only ones that God anoints in the Old Testament. The anointing is a type of a qualifying component for ministry and service on which these three groups are people who serve in specific reason, serving God for a higher purpose. This anointing is the ability to do the work of God: as Creflo A Dollar mentioned in one of his teachings; the Holy Spirit is "the empowerment for the assignment."

In Acts 10:28- Jesus functioned in that anointing to heal all who were oppressed by the Devil and went about doing good things. God anoints those He calls and uses them under that Power. The anointing can also be described as the presence and essence of God. It is God Himself. It is impossible to separate God from the anointing. He is the anointing. The ones who are allowed to enter into the Holiest of all are the ones that have been ordained to partake in the anointing, the Presence of God, the power of the Holy Spirit.

The Blood and the Anointing

When God through Jesus tore down the veil that separates and accepts every distinct party, He was actually telling the world that He has eventually anointed every one that is now willing to accept Jesus. Notice Jesus is mentioned here in this statement and, why? It is His blood that had caused paradise to be no more, for when Jesus rose from the dead He took with Him the believing folks that were waiting upon the day when Heaven will open the door to them.

Heaven was not opened to them because the Angels have finally finished building the city of Heaven, No! It was opened for them because the blood has been shed, the ransom has been paid for and this has earned them the right to come into the presence of the Father. Glory to God for His mercy! The blood of Jesus opens the way for Humans to come back to the Father. It is the qualifying component to stand before God. Once an individual has been justified through the blood and he or she has access to the presence of God, then the presence of God or the anointing from God that resides in him or her becomes the qualifying component to serve God before Man.

In summary to this chapter: **"the blood is the qualifying component for one to come before God shameless, and the anointing from God is the qualifying component to serve God before His people and the World".**

If God has also accepted and anointed everybody including the women, then the issue would be that God would use women to speak in the Churches, to teach Sunday school, to Pastor Churches and even to head companies. Their only exclusion is that they are not anointed to be head over the man. Man remains the head of the wife. There are some men who would not allow Women preachers. My question to these men is: What rights have you to be a qualifying candidate to speak and preach for God? What have you that the woman does not have?

The anointing is what makes you a qualifying candidate to speak for God. There is nothing special about you, only the fact that you are anointed. If God has also anointed women, what right have you to judge them whether or not they should speak? They have the qualifying element to be qualified candidates to speak for God. What God has approved, let no man treat otherwise.

Pay careful attention to this scripture.

Joel 2:28- "And it shall come to pass afterward that I will pour out My Spirit on all flesh; Your sons and daughters shall prophesy, Your old men shall dream dreams, Your young men shall see visions. 29-And also on my menservants and on my maidservants I will pour out My Spirit in those days. (NKJV)

The promise of God came to pass when Jesus died, the veils were broken and the Spirit was poured on all flesh regardless of gender or race; everyone is now able to receive the Spirit, the anointing of God. Verse 28 tells us that your sons and **daughters** shall **prophesy.** The root word for "prophesy" in these passages according to the original Greek, "Naba", means, "speak under the inspiration". Wow! Isn't that what we been trying to establish, doesn't that confirm all we've been talking about? Women given the green light to speak for God and be heard just like the men!

This is an absolute contradiction to that earlier teaching that limits women from speaking in the Churches, whereas over here in this passage we find that after resurrection and the giving of the Holy Spirit the women are now given the right to speak, preach and proclaim in the Churches. But why is there a direct contradiction?

Well, Paul was speaking of this matter based on his understanding of the Old Order. The New Order that begins with the death, burial and resurrection of Jesus has approved the women of all races to speak and be heard, to be that significant somebody that God has called them to be. Your daughters, the women of our day have all the right in the world to speak and be heard, the awesome right to be somebody. Verse 29 of the living bible states that God has poured out

His Spirit even on the Slaves, which tells us that even the lowest of all classes has been anointed of the Spirit of God; they have what it takes to get the Job done.

As we have heard earlier that women are classified along with slaves and Gentiles. According to our study of the temple, they are the farthest away from the Holy of Holies, the room of God's habitation. It was after the outpouring of the Mighty Holy Spirit during Pentecost that Peter pinpointed some very startling truths to his audience.

Acts 2:38- Then Peter said to them, " Repent and let every one of you be baptized in the Name of Jesus Christ for the remission of sins; and you shall receive the Holy Spirit as a gift. 39- "For the promise is to you and to your children, and to all who are afar off, as many as the Lord our God will call."

So what do we see; the ones afar off have now been anointed by God with the Spirit of God. They have been qualified and justified by God Almighty. Who are the ones afar off from the Holiest according to our study of the Temple? They are the Women and the Gentile World.

Whew! Jump and rejoice for you all can be what God wants for you to be, and Christ really smiles to see you finding out about your true freedom in Christ Jesus.

THE YOKES OF RELIGIOUS TRADITION DESTROYED

GALATIANS 5: 1-It is for freedom Christ has set us free stand firm then and do not be burdened again by a yoke of slavery.

The first line of that verse reads that freedom was the reason Christ came to set us free. Our Heavenly Father sent Jesus His Son to set us free because He loves us so much He wants us to enjoy living in freedom. Now notice for a moment the second portion of that verse that reads; "by a yoke of slavery", is singular and not plural. The burden comes by a yoke, one only and the burden are felt therefore the many the yokes of bondage upon a person's life, the heavier the burden is going to be felt. Let me give you a connection in this next verse:

ISAIAH 10:27- And it shall come to pass in that day, that his burden shall be taken away from thy shoulder, and his yoke from thy neck, and the yoke shall be destroyed because of the Anointing.

The last portion of that verse says that the yoke is destroyed because of the anointing, what it does not say though is the anointing destroying the burden. God does not destroy burdens. He destroys yokes because yokes are the cause of the burdens. If the yoke is upon a neck of a person or an animal then the burden, pressure, weight, stress, so on and so forth will be felt on the shoulder area and downwards. That is probably the reason why when people are under so much stress, they need a good shoulder massage and sometimes it works. Thank God for massage therapists! However the yokes that are still there need to be dealt with.

As long as a yoke of slavery is upon one's life, the burden will be felt upon his neck and shoulder area. As soon as that yoke is destroyed by the power of the anointing, the burden is lifted and ultimately removed whereby freedom can be enjoyed. Ah! A sigh of relief! What is a yoke? It is simply a thought pattern that manifests itself through the behavior of one's life, a corruptive thought producing a limiting behavior.

The power of God (anointing) through knowledge destroys these yokes and burdens are removed, sometimes automatically and other times progressively. These yokes of slavery range from addictions, bad habits, a suppressing system and most of all, the very cause of it all, a corruptive thinking pattern. How a person feels is due to how he or she permits his/her mind to think.

If we think good thoughts we'll feel good and eventually do well. As we go back to verse 2 of Galatians 5, we locate the single yoke he was talking about and that is the religious tradition of circumcision. Circumcision when taken legalistically, it becomes a yoke and a burden! How can it be? If God was the one who instituted these religious traditions and observance, why is it then an instrument of bondage and burden rather than freedom and joy?

Well, along with the tradition about women not having a say, all the other religious ones that God Almighty instituted were truly blessed by God and were meant to only guide the Jewish people only up to the new order of things that begun on the death, burial and resurrection of Jesus Christ. Any tradition that is still observed and exercised after resurrection is simply religion without power.

It has lost its sacredness after the new order is put in force, and to continue to observe them is to bring only bondage and burden. In Galatians 5-2 Paul states that to walk according to these traditions is to not see the full effect and benefit of the Christ, to fall from His grace. The Greek for the Name Christ is "Christos", and the Hebrew is "Messiah" for which both give us the same meaning: "The Anointed One and His Anointing." To not see the effects and benefits of Christ is to live a life of religion without the Anointing Power of God in manifestation.

That is pure dead religion denying the Power thereof. Are their Churches that are just like that? Of course! There are religions and Churches that introduce yokes, burden, bondage and boredom more than freedom and joy. These religions and even churches dish out certain rules for you to live by, having based their doctrines and rules according to the old knowledge of the Old Covenant or some human cultural tradition for the religious sects.

They'd have to dress a certain way, hair do's a certain way, restrictions placed upon some as to who should and should not speak in the Churches. Then there are those who cannot express love through blood donation, then the others who observe special days and Holy days along with the restrictions of eating certain foods. Gosh, the list goes on and on! Visit these religions, and you just want to get out of that circle as quick as possible; you feel more bound than free. Am I saying that they don't have the power of the anointing of God as what they are supposed to have?

Not at all, I believe all Christians have the Power of the Anointing regardless, but not all Christians get to see the benefits and effects of it. These religious, legalistic rules and regulations only put lids upon the Spirits container who is the human spirit, the residency of the Holy Spirit. These (religious traditions) suppress the Holy Spirit inside that container from manifesting Himself and doing marvelous and wondrous things. Wait a minute! Are you saying the Holy Spirit can be stopped? Absolutely! If you would not let Him move He won't! The Holy Spirit is a Gentleman and will not in any way, shape or form, force Himself in even though He has all Powers.

The Christian who lives with a certain principle that is legalistic still does have the Power of the Holy Spirit but has contained the Him (Holy Spirit) inside the container (human spirit). It is a position of limiting the Holy Spirit from demonstrating His Power in that particular area of his/her life. Sugar in the pot does not sweeten the cup of tea; it's when the sugar is scooped from the pot to the cup of tea that sweetens the Tea.

As I have said earlier, the human spirit is just the container for the Holy Spirit and the Holy Spirit can be restricted and contained in His container without affecting the world around us. He can live inside of us but we would be failing to experience healing in our bodies, failing to experience the blessing of our pockets and bank accounts or deliverance from demonic activity or bad habits. I may not tell you today of what scoops up power from the inside out, but I sure will tell you of one specific lid that contains Him, and that is, religious tradition.

I have personally seen Christians who become spiritual weirdo's practicing religious traditions that's been done away with two thousand years ago. Religions traditions have lost its sacredness and power. This is pure legalism and bondage, a form of religion denying the power thereof.

Have you hung around Christian people who act like that? It is an uneasy feeling. A feeling of criticism and condemnation is always in the air where the people are always trying to be good because they are always feeling not good enough. If you live in the liberty of the Spirit, to them you are probably from Hell or are possessed with the spirit of Jezebel.

What I am talking about is the fact that these groups of Gods people strive to practice external ordinances and rules to feel accepted and they are always criticizing themselves for not being good enough, and so they criticize others for not living up to that standard as well. The way we treat ourselves is the way we will treat others. I've actually seen some men wear long sleeve shirts in hot and muggy summer weather. They forbid the wearing of short sleeve T Shirts. It's crazy! No wonder the people of the World calls the Christians crazy. I guess one would say God has all kinds on His side, the good the bad and the ugly. Which one are you?

CHAPTER FOURTEEN

Cry Freedom!

Part of God's original plan for mankind is freedom enjoyed and the way that is experienced is through responsibility. The responsible individual is someone who protects the freedom given, and not the person who misuses or abuses it. After God created Adam and Eve, He then shared authority with Adam to be in charge with everything in their possession. God gave them full responsibility of what was in their possession. They had both the freedom to execute their choices, and the responsibility to make good choices.

Freedom can only be preserved through responsibility. He (God) created us as free moral agents where we get to choose what we want whatever life we desire to live and God is in no position to change that choice. It is the consequences of the choices we make that we will have to live with or the benefits of good healthy choices. Adam and Eve misused that freedom by making irresponsible choices that not only affect them, but the whole world after them. You as a woman of God have the freedom of choice that can either make you free or more bound.

The realization of your freedom that comes through Jesus' death, burial and resurrection is only the first step into enjoying this freedom; you will have to make solid choices that lead to action and then results. Your choice today is so critical because it will lead to consequences or benefits that will directly or indirectly affect yourself and the people you love. You can choose to stay afraid or put action to your newfound knowledge that will literally change your life forever.

Choices inspired by knowledge and the responsibility of one's life that is ever ready to break borders of religion, culture or traditional customs. When you do, all Heaven will show up because it is the word that you are obeying and not some humanistic teaching. This binding tradition that enslaves people's lives regardless of race, gender or color has invaded the existence of human kind and impacted it so negatively that women become shut out and shut down from their true potential.

It comes in many shapes and sizes but the bottom line is, "they have no Say." After recognizing the partial understanding of the Apostle Paul in this specific area due to the progressive nature of revelation, and recognizing through what we've learnt in this study the complete works of the cross of Jesus which provided the total freedom of all women, it will take absolute courage and responsibility to act like it is so. Courage for the women to be the person they were created to be and to boldly come forth with a voice because there will be religious, cultural and gender opposition and criticism.

One has to be responsible enough to act out realizing that it is not only going to affect them today, but also their children and children's children tomorrow. Actions inspired by accurate and sound knowledge that will bombard and penetrate through the barricades of discriminations, which have been standing from generation to generation, limiting the woman of all time. These actions will eventually change the way women are treated in the future; the responsible choice will attain the freedom desired.

I urge you woman of God to walk in that freedom and continue to, even when the stakes are high, even if the denomination you are a member of does not accept woman preachers or leaders. Continue to walk in this freedom even if it means making new enemies, just go ahead and make new friends too.

New friends are not too far away, you'll be surprised how many friends that are out there who are going the way you are going, who believe what you believe, becoming that significant somebody that God's created you to be. Go where you are celebrated, not where you are tolerated! There are churches, ministries and peoples who are more than willing to celebrate your gifts and truly benefit from it, get attached to them!

That will be considered responsible choice, choices that will literally elevate the treatment of women in the Churches and of course amongst your children and children's children. For tomorrow to change, it would take radical acts springing out from responsible choices by women who have found out the truth and have decided that they should put an end to this out-dated knowledge that puts limits to the woman of our day, "enough is enough" is the cry for freedom.

REDEEMED FROM LIFELESS TRADITIONS

Jesus' blood has already paid for our freedom from traditions that are negative and demeaning; they are cultures and even systems of entire countries and continents. Systems that absorb life out of Humans, the ones that dehydrate the meaning of life from the existence of Humanity in all ages, but we've always seen the fall of systems that do more harm than good. God is against such systems or traditions.

Communism is a system, and communism is a system that Jesus has already set people free from. Racism is a system, and racism is a system that Jesus has already set people free from.

Terrorism is a system, and terrorism is a system that Jesus has already set people free from.

It is like the Bill of Rights, it'll need to be taken advantage of for it to be enjoyed personally. No matter what freedom Christ has already purchased, someone has got to rise up and take advantage of the freedom provided. It's not going to come easy, it will not go down without a fight, but it will succeed because God is backing it up 100%. I believe that God fully backed Ronald Reagan on his stand against Communism and the fall of the Iron Curtain.

I believe that God fully backed Martin Luther King Jr on his stand against racism and His fight for freedom and equal rights for the African Americans. I believe that God is behind a nation like the United States, a President like George Bush that fights to bring terrorism to its knees, and terrorism will definitely be subdued and brought to justice! Imprisonment was the price of the fight against the apartheid in South Africa for which Nelson Mandela had served a total of twenty years.

These are not political statements but statements of freedom, for freedom is won by war whereas injustice is made concrete through the basis of permission. Whatever we tolerate we make strong. But these men have demonstrated an attitude that do not condone such injustices and have pledged their lives for the pulling down of strongholds.

What these men have in common is a cry for freedom, a holy hatred for an oppressing system, a fervent and burning passion to end this ridiculous culture, system, tradition or whatever you would want to call it. These great men change history. They with a lot of courage and their love for the human race have demonstrated by their actions God's Holy truth being practically applied. Whether knowingly or not, they are all that and more, they are definitely world changers!

When you, a woman of God decide to act upon the knowledge of God and refuse to be oppressed by a system that limits you, you can be rest assured to expect the same results as these great men have. It's going to take a fight, it will take a while but if you with the knowledge of Jesus work on the Cross will act like it is so, it will be. Peter reveals from his writings the awesome freedom through the blood of Jesus.

I Peter 1-18 Knowing that you were not redeemed with corruptible things, like Silver or Gold, from your aimless conduct received by tradition from your fathers, 19: but with the precious blood of Christ, as of a Lamb without blemish and without spot.

Verse 19 says; the blood of the Lamb has redeemed us, and from what? Verse 20 tells us that we have been redeemed from behaviors that are aimless and empty and only absorb life out of us, traditions handed down by our forefathers from generation to generation. The blood of Jesus is shed to set us free from any tradition that is negative and destructive.

The woman deprived of their true identity and potential is a negative and destructive tradition to which our Lord Jesus has already taken care away when he died. To some it may be their religious traditional belief, to others a cultural traditional belief or whatever roots of background it may have. His (Jesus) blood has already purchased the freedom required and it's all up to us to reinforce the freedom.

Reinforcing this freedom is to live like it is so, you have a voice and you can be what God's called you to be in Christ Jesus.   Reinforcing it is to simply pass on this new tradition to your friends, to your colleagues and especially to your children and   children's children.

IT IS FOR FREEDOM CHRIST HAS SET US FREE

Why does God intend for us to be free? So we can enjoy life being free. God sets people free not so that they can serve Him but so that the people can enjoy Freedom. No strings attached, He just wants the best for everyone so they can live free. To serve Him is a by-product of being free and an essential element for staying free.

What do I mean by service being a by-product of being free? As soon as people begin to enjoy freedom by Christ, the next big thing that comes along is the desire to serve Him and eventually the attitude of gratitude. Even then our service does not benefit God because He maneuvers our service toward serving people. Jesus said; "what you've done for the least of these, you have done to me."

God loves the World so much that even when we call it serving God, it's just directed to serving people. Amazing! Isn't it, The God who changes lives simply doing it for the sake of "LOVE", and that He just wants the best for every human being but, unfortunately, not every human being will accept His great love?

With all the rejection of one type of freedom by human kind, their cravings for freedom of another kind still persist. Ask any inmate? He'll tell you how much he longs for freedom. Ask any woman from the Islam faith? She'll tell you the longing for freedom she has. Ask any religious person who observes legalistic rules and bondage? He'll tell you of his silent inner cry for freedom. What have humankind in common? They all want to be free!

What about the Jewish Women?

It has been told by most Christian people who also believe in what I believe, women having the right to speak and be heard, that the only reason Paul had said the things he said about women was that he was only talking to the Jewish people and not the Gentiles and then their explanation comes to an end, period. If that was the answer than what we are really saying is that this bondage is not for the Gentiles, only the Jews. Is it?

This leaves us with unanswered questions for the truth about Women. The earlier chapters of this book reveal to us that the Apostle Paul was actually directing his message to the Church regardless of what race encompasses all the Churches. To Timothy he stated; "I do not permit a woman to speak in the Churches, period." What he didn't say though was; I do not permit the Jewish woman in your Church to speak. Imagine how degrading it would be, if in a Church consisting Jews and Gentiles that only the Christian Jews are supposed to observe that.

If that was the case, then I can boldly say that God cannot be the preacher of Diversity in Unity but in reality, God is the author of Diversity in Unity. Paul based upon partial understanding of revelation decreed that all women should abide in this rule, regardless of what race. However, as we have already established, this freedom has come to all including the Jewish women.

God would not permit a single race to live like this, not even the Jews. Gosh! Don't you think the Jewish people also have feelings? They are humans too. They crave freedom just like any other human being on the face of this earth.

Don't tell me that Paul's teaching is only meant for the Jews because the Jews, too, hate to live in bondage, therefore they also want out of the whole theory that woman are to be silent in the Church and especially when a Jew has become a Christian.

Thank God for the Christ who has brought positive changes to the world! If one group of people wants out of these types of shackles, every other group wants out as well. It is freedom they all want. God has not meant for only a certain group of people to live like that, not even the Jews.

Ordinances enforced for reason of keeping order.

During a period of time before Jesus' death on the cross for reasons of order was this ordinance decreed that it be observed, but not anymore and not supposed to after the new order of things which begun at the Cross. There is now no difference between a Jew and a Gentile. Galatians 3-29.

CHAPTER FIFTEEN

Renewed To the New Order

Even after the awesome understanding of God's will concerning women that came through the death, burial and resurrection of Jesus which we had established in chapters nine, ten and eleven of this book, real and concrete change will not come that easy for most of us. I had to remind and challenge my wife to her new identity, especially when someone observes this old identity as a traditional culture of her native people.

Learning and understanding of truth doesn't mean change. Change comes through acceptance of truth and acting upon it; it takes involvement for change to happen. It all begins with the understanding part of it and the daily repetition of the same knowledge over in our mind or Soul realm.

The old identity and behavior of one's life resides in his/her mind; it has been programmed in his/her mind to act in a certain way. The only way to change the behavior part is to first change the thinking part. The writer of Hebrews says about Jesus complete mission as the setting up of a new order that both Jews and Gentiles should live by and also the taking away of the old order or system. (Hebrews: 910).

This new order is the manifestation of the Image of God himself whereby when we see the system, we are seeing God. God is expressed and revealed to us through the equal rights of male and female and the eradication of gender, religious discrimination or any other form of discrimination. In Colossians-3: 10- the word putting on the new man tells us of this Christian life that we have   begun to live by when we are born again and this new life operates in a new order or system.

Also the word "renewed in knowledge according to the image of the Creator" gives us the idea that this new man to live by the new order, he has to be renewed according to the image of God as according to this passage found in verse 11.

After concluding from verse 10 with the Image of God, verse 11 begins with "where there is neither Greek nor Jew, circumcised nor uncircumcised, Barbarian, Scythian, slave nor free but Christ is all in all." Notice the **"where"** in verse 11 points to the **Image of God** which is verse 10. Verse 11 reveals that the Image of God, the where he's talking about harbors no discrimination, prejudice or favoritism. Praise the Lord!

There is no double standard in God, for in His image there is no discrimination. I cannot get it in my thick skull how in the World is it possible for groups such as the KKK to preach Jesus as Savior and yet shout from the rooftop the hate message of discrimination! The Image of God is; "for God so Love the World", no particular race, color or gender mentioned. Praise God forever more!

Paul did not mention the gender issue here when he mentions equality as opposed to his words in Galatians 3: 29 where equality of Gender was mentioned. Why didn't he speak of it over here in his letter to the Ephesians what he mentioned to the Galatians? Well, one does not write word for word everything he has written in the past what he writes in this other letter. Only mass production companies do that. Paul's letters are personal.

This is somewhat like the synoptic Gospels, they speak the same things but different wordings, terminology used is different and in some instances, they add just a little bit more than what the other does not reveal. He wrote this based on what his audience needs to know and what truths his audience already knew. The theory of gender equality can be proven because the author writes the same theory in his letters to the other Churches where he not only mentions races and status but the gender issue too.

The synoptic Gospels, Mathew, Mark and Luke who provide information just a little bit different from the other, a little bit of abstracts from here and there but as you put their stories and information together then it will begin to make sense. It's more like saying the same thing but with different wordings, different versions and what information that would seem fit for them to use depending upon what their audience is like. Paul when writing to the Galatians Church included the Gender equality.

Galatians 3:28-There is neither Jew nor Greek, there is neither slave nor free, there is neither Male nor Female; for you are all one in Christ Jesus.

It does make sense that in the Image of God there is no prejudice, or any form of discrimination. We are to renew our minds to that awesome Image of God where our diversity is celebrated, accepted, treated equally with the same enjoyed rights, benefits and privileges rather than being disregarded, discriminated and pushed away as nothing. It is truly sad that we still have ministers who treat Women differently from the way of the new order of things.

Some religions of the world and Christian Churches still will not accept women ministers such as Joyce Meyer, Marilyn Hickey, Gloria Copeland and many more like them. Could it be that these church religious people have un-renewed minds? Could it be that these so-called people's cultures and religions operate in un-renewed mindsets? I believe so! If truly our minds

76

are renewed then we will see them the way God sees them and accept them in their true identity, being the women leaders of our day.

Accepting them according to their true identity that came by the death, burial and resurrection of Jesus and to see them with a new vision that they do have a say in this world would mean making room for them to prosper in their role and calling. To renew our minds to the Image of God is to possess a vision of diversity in race, culture and gender, possessing a vision for different roles and responsibility but equal rights and benefits as a Human being and as a child of God.

This is God's perception of the Human race. Renewing your mind to that awesome Image of God is to put these truths in your mind, in your mouth and even act like it is so. If you are a woman of God, begin to walk in that wonderful privilege of being a voice in your Church and in whatever professional world you may be called to, by not letting any to deprive you of such blessing. Choose your Church, friends and even your job if that is what it takes to have an environment that contributes to the renewing of your mind to the Image of God.

I Timothy 4-12-Let no man-look down on you because you are young,

Let no man look down on you is the same sentence as let the pets out of the house or let the kids outdoor for recreation. The word **"Let"** implies that whoever is doing the letting is the one with the power and not the cat or the kid. It is the same with this verse. When people look down on us, it is because we let them, we give them the go ahead to look down on us and despise us. We empower them to do so. If we can give them the power to look down and despise us, we can also give them the power to look up at us and esteem highly of us.

We set ourselves in the place of Gods exaltation, our true identity, as a woman who has been given the right to be a voice in the Church and whatever place of public or private ministry there is.

Just walk in it! Live in it! Enjoy it!

CHAPTER SIXTEEN

Behind every successful Man is a Woman Who has a say.

It's been said that behind every successful man is a powerful woman, but I say; **"Behind every successful man is a woman who is allowed to speak."** Notice I didn't use the word "nagging." Wives can nag and break their husbands or they can build them up with words that are full of respect and love. It's not always the best option to get the job done; "ladies" there is a better way. Ephesians 5: 33 say's that wives ought to give their husbands the respect due them.

When you respect your boss your own words will tell, you will never run your boss down by your words, it will be the exemption of mean talk, trash talk, nagging and threatening type talk. You will be watchful over what proceeds out of your mouth. You'd make sure that if you say a thing it would be for the betterment of the company. You would rather say constructive words than destructive. In the same way, if wives truly respect their husbands, their words will tell it all.

They will not nag, threaten or say words that run and degrade their husband's, rather they will say words that are constructive and definitely showing respect. They are careful in watching over what proceeds out of their mouth. The only difference between the respects we give is one, we owed to our boss, and to the other, we want for our husbands. So here we understand that I am not encouraging wives to despise their husbands, but to say whatever it is that need to be said in a more respectful and constructive manner.

Genesis 2: 18 say's that the woman was known to be the Helpmeet for the Man. I think the role of a woman is somewhat similar to the role of the Mighty Holy Spirit because the Holy Spirit is also known to be the one who is sent to help.

John –15: 26 "But when the Helper comes, whom I shall send to you from the Father, the Spirit of truth who proceeds from the Father, He will testify of Me.

The Helper, the Holy Spirit helps by means of speaking. The last part portion of that Scripture says that the Spirit testifies, speaks and in this fashion helps. Wives being the helper, they also help in the same way, by means of speaking life into the lives of their husbands. They aid and assist in other ways as well but one significant way they do that is by what they say. She has the capacity to make or break her husband by her attitude and definitely by her mouth. A woman who carelessly speaks over her husband has no doubt very little respect for him.

The basic personality of every woman is to be a caretaker whereas the basic personality of all man is to be a risk-taker. She wants security, safety and support. He wants to give support, provide security and safety and therefore takes risks. Sometimes she will have to trust her husband when he feels it's a risk worth taking; she'll choose to submit even if she doesn't understand. She'll say that which will boost him to initiate, to continue or to finish the race. Other times, she'll need to speak up and save her husband from a foolish venture. She, being the helper, the caretaker, will speak life to her soul mate, her partner in life.

I've done many things that I later regretted, and one reason was by not giving heed to the helpmeet that was assigned for my success, my wonderful friend and wife. How much easier and safer it would be for men, had they tapped into the great potential and wisdom of their spouses. I'd say to men, "listen to your wives and let them voice the help that you desperately crave for". It's about time. Avoid the pitfalls by drawing from your wives great and invaluable help.

Some men are hesitant in giving them the power to do so, the power to speak and be heard probably for reasons of being afraid of losing power and control. Most men fear women because of verbal abuse, hence fear develops and escalates into lying and a weak character. Most men speak lies to their wives and sometimes almost unconsciously without any guilt whatsoever for fear of verbal abuse and condemnation. You might be saying, "She doesn't respect me, why should I let her speak into my life". How do I get her to respect me and speak constructively to me, to only say words that build? To only say words of respect.

MEN – LOVE LIKE JESUS LOVED

Men do not need to shut down women for fear of abuse, for fear of losing power and authority because when they do so, they'd be shutting down help and resources. Men don't need to close the door to the ministry of help for reasons of fear and insecurity, when there is bible help to get the women to turn around their influence from breaking to making.

When we see a negative bent in influence, it is important to recognize the positive influence trying to manifest and that it was buried and corrupted with the negatives of life. It is simply a gift given to women for positive purposes but through life's setbacks, traumatic incidents and disappointments, a gift becomes corrupted. That gift can produce tremendous-making or disastrous-breaking in the life of those closest to them especially the husbands and children.

A man of Understanding will pull the best out.

Proverbs 20: 5- Counsel in the heart of man is like deep water, but a man of understanding will draw it out.

To understand what women have within them is one thing, but to further understand how to draw from them is surely another thing. This next passage of scripture teaches us something about the women.

Proverbs 30:21-22-23 – Three things cause the earth to tremble and four it cannot bear: a servant when he reigns, a fool when he is filled with food, a hateful woman when she is married and a maidservant who succeeds her mistress.

One of the four things that cause the world to tremble according to that Scripture is a hateful woman when she gets married. Some translation says; "an unloved woman when she is married", which reveals a woman who hasn't been loved like she ought to, respected like she ought to will manifest her gift in a negative and destructive manner.

I've personally seen Pastors' wives who don't support their husbands and everyone in the congregation would be so quick to judge her. In most cases that I have personally dealt with, it would be that the wife is playing up because she is not happy. She's not happy because she is not getting it. Her actions are visibly saying something. Once the husband is able to see that and meets it, she eventually will crawl out of the cocoon she has been lying in for who knows how long.

When a woman is married, she will be looking for love in that relationship, and if she doesn't find it, she will demand for it even in a negative and destructive manner. And probably sometimes look for it elsewhere. This is the same with kids and husbands and every human being on the Earth; they are waiting to be found! Gary Chapman, author of the Love languages series speaks in details regarding these factors.

Questions most men will probably be asking. What if the woman I'm married to has been looking for love almost all her single life and does not find it? Disrespected and unappreciated by the world she was exposed to? I show love and respect to her but she keeps on living the way she does, so now my patience is running out and I'm beginning to retaliate and hold grudges.

I believe that she has to show me respect and submit herself to me as according to the Bible. What do I have to say to her to make her change her life? It's not what you need to say to her, it's what you have to show by your actions. Show love and respect with consistency even if there is still no sign of a turnaround. Notice these words of Paul:

Ephesians 5: 25 – Husbands love your wives, just as Christ also love the Church and gave himself for her, 26 that he might sanctify and cleanse her with the washing of water by the word.

Paul is comparing the relationship between Christ and the Church as similar to relationships between husbands and wives. Notice the last line to verse 25 is Christ giving of himself to the Church which best describes our turnaround. We were sinners, lovers of the world, haters of God and immoral in every way, but Christ loved us first. Romans 5: 8- states that God loved us first before we even loved Him. It's our recognition of that love that leads us to repentance. In the same way with our relationship to our wives as husbands, we need to show, demonstrate through our actions our passionate and consistent love for our wives.

I've come to see this to be true with my relationship to my wife is that no matter how hard I try to get her to submit to my vision and plans; they just drive her farther away from me - my vision and plans. I've started this principle over the years and have come to see lasting rewards, my wife has taken the turnaround and is very supportive and in total agreement with my vision and plans. I took the first steps of loving her and in return she is submissive to my role as the head of this relationship.

I would give of myself tirelessly and wholeheartedly; I would operate with a spirit of love to serve and worship her, I'd go the second mile just to treat her like a princess she is. Today, I love her more, she submits more. You want a happy life? Give your wife a happy one. The principle is, "Happy wife, Happy Life". She does not care what you know and are capable off, not until she knows you really care for her and how she feels will she change. Listening to her talk and expressing herself is one way of showing love and care.

What will make her the woman of God she ought to be lies in your hands as the head of the wife, and as the head of the family. If you, as a husband, would love unconditionally, you would definitely dig past the negative carnal attitudes to bring out the best in her. The best lies within. Listen to them and let them speak!

CHAPTER SEVENTEEN

To see Jesus is to see the Father

Whatever Jesus was and is the Father is also. Jesus healed the sick the Father heals the sick, Jesus Loves people the Father loves people. The two never contradict, but the only place you will see them working differently is when they have different roles. Different roles one goal! Jesus mentioned these in His own words; **"If you've seen me you've seen the Father" John 14: 9,** and this next verse just blows my mind away because we New Testament believers, tend to think that the God of the Old Testament is a mean guy.

Watch the next verses of the Scripture by Jesus' own words.

John 16: 26- 27

In that day you will ask in my name, and I do not say to you that I shall pray the Father for you; for the Father Himself loves you, because you have loved me, and believe that I came forth from God.

Jesus said; after talking about praying in His name that He does not pray to the Father for us to get the Father to do things for us, but the Father Himself loves us, and is not needed to be persuaded by the son to do so. The "FATHER" Himself loves you and wants to do things for you! That's why He sent His son to die on the cross so we can have a relationship with Him and enjoy the benefits of the Son of God. Paul says in His letter to the Romans that we are heirs of God and co- heir with the Son. This tells us that we share in the benefits with our big brother; "Jesus Christ the Lord." It is true that when we see how the SON OF GOD behaves in this World over two thousand years ago we are seeing the Father. Jesus is the exact representative of the Godhead bodily! Glory to His Name forever!

Colossians 2: 9- For in Him dwells all the fullness of the Godhead bodily.

Do not be deceived into thinking that the God of the Old Testament is a mean God. If He were mean, then Jesus would be too, but Jesus wasn't mean and neither is the Father! The Godhead represented by Jesus showed incredible love to the Women.

Woman with Issue of Blood

The Woman with issue of blood touched Jesus with her hand. According to the Law, she violated two laws; the first was, approaching a Rabbai, secondly coming into the public for they were forbidden to do that while having the issue of blood. No wonder she was afraid when Jesus inquired as to whom touched her. Jesus' response after she owned up was; "Cheer Up". That is God's response to all women, no matter what level of impurity there is. Luke 9:43-48

Sinful Woman in the house of Simon

A sinful woman that came and wet the Lord's feet with her tears, dried them with her hair, and anointed them with oil, was judged by Pharisees who were there to dine with the Lord. Not only was she judged for being a sinner. Jesus was judged more for not knowing who she was, when in fact the Pharisees expected of Him to know since He was a prophet. This woman probably was a prostitute because one would be a sinner, were she to sleep with many men. With all that being said, I would like to point out a rather interesting observation. Verse 39 of Luke 7 states two inquiring and judgmental thoughts by Simon. The judgmental thoughts were:

1. Jesus should know who she is:

2. Jesus should know what manner of person she is:

    Who is this? A Woman

    What manner of person? A sinner

Again, Jesus violated the laws by letting a Woman approach and touch Him, and also because she was a sinner. Before Jesus took away the laws that restricted Israel and the Gentile World upon the cross on a universal level, He dealt with them individually as He encounters them. He worked on the Sabbath which was a total contradiction to the law, and even quotes that the Father God works: "John 5: 16- 17." Jesus disciples' ate with dirty hands and were accused for violating the law. Jesus corrected them as He brought to their understanding the New Testament theology, that what they were observing was the shadow of reality. He lets Women come to Him!

Woman served in His ministry

There were women seen in the ministry of Jesus at all times. Another violation! We see them serving Him with their substance and were following the team of evangelizing everywhere. (Luke 8: 1- 3)

The first evangelists that preached the resurrection of the Lord Jesus were woman. (Luke 24: 1- 11)

Jesus not only let women come into His presence, but also to serve with their substance and even preached the resurrection!

THE GREAT EXCHANGE

Under the New Covenant upon which we stand everything we enjoy and live by is solely based upon what Jesus died for. In His death everything we get to enjoy today was paid for by His Blood and made available to us as an exchange for something negative in our lives. Ponder upon these wonderful truths:

The Son of God became the Son of man so Sons of man can become Sons of God.

He who had no sin became sin for us so we can become the righteousness of God in Christ.

He became a curse for us so we can be blessed in the blessings of Abraham.

He took up our infirmities, made sick so we can be healed and live in good health.

He became poor for our sakes so that in His poverty we might become rich.

He was rejected and despised so that those who have been rejected, discriminated, pushed away and despised by the society, a race or gender can all become one and equal in Christ Jesus despite their differences.

May the good Lord raise you up as a human being and may you accept His perception of you. May He continue to rise up mighty women of valor in these last days just as He has been doing throughout the History of the World!

Bibliographies

The Story of the New Testament: John Stott and revised by Stephen Motyer. First published in the USA in 2001 by Baker Books a division of Baker Book House Company P O Box 6287, Grand Rapids, MI 49516-6287

The revenge of Ephesus: Dr Joseph B Fuiten. Copyright 2005.

Senior Pastor of Cedar Park Assembly of God and founder of Cedar Park Christians Schools

Gods Generals, why they succeeded and why some failed: Roberts Liardon Printed in the United States. 1030Hunt Valley Circle New Kensington, PA 15068 Whitaker House

The Spirit Within & The Spirit upon: Kenneth E. Hagin Copyright 2003. Rhema Bible Church AKA Kenneth Hagin Ministries Inc. All rights reserved Printed in the USA

NKJV Copyright 1982 by Thomas Nelson, Inc The Maxwell leadership Bible: John C. Maxwell.

Other sources of Bible and Concordance used:

New International Version/Zondervan Study Bible, New Living Bible Translation, Amplified Bible/ Zondervan, Strongs Analytical Concordance

About the Author

Bruce Kele was born in the Fiji islands and has moved to the United States of America in September of 2001 with his wife and three kids. His fourth child was born in the US. He has been pastor of two different churches in the past fourteen years. Bruce is a gifted teacher of the Word of God and a motivational speaker. His ministry outreaches cover the pacific Islands where he has travelled extensively to countries such as Tonga, Western and American samoa as well as Australia. He is currenttly ministering as a travelling minister in Canada while completing a Masters degree in transformational leadership.

Printed in the United States
by Baker & Taylor Publisher Services